More Pr ... ed!

"Extremely interesti ... book that can be used on all levels ... of excitement will help you achieve the goal of Spectacular Customer Service. The enthusiasm of the ideas grasp the reader and demand to be enthusiastically implemented. A great book!"
Gareth Ackerman, Deputy Chairman, Pick 'n Pay

"South Africans stand accused of getting the service they deserve. Juiced! is a must read for those who are tired of taking it. It tells you what you have the right to expect in Customer Service, but more importantly, it tells those who have been dashing our expectations all these years how to do something about it."
Theo Garrun, Editor, The Star Workplace

"Very practical and useful."
Dr Fanus Gouws, Rapport

"Juiced! is an outstanding book with clear, easy to follow, practical suggestions, ideas and sparks. It is motivational...very much my kind of reading. In particular, I appreciated the idea of being able to recap the experience through the summary. I found that once the idea was there I only needed to read the summary line to remind me of the value. I became Juiced! ...and Juicy."
Martin Bailie, Radio Cape Talk 567

"In order to prosper in the global economy, the level of service in South Africa has to reach international standards. This book is a guide on how to do the basics and so motivate your staff in the right direction."
Michael Mark, CEO, Truworths Ltd.

"A uniquely fresh approach to Spectacular Customer Service. Easy to read, but powerful."
Ronnie Stein, Group Financial Director, the Foschini Group.

"The passion of the authors is infectious, and will infect your organisation with a passion for service!"
Philip Krawitz, Chairman, Cape Union Mart Group

"A racy, humorous and practical guide – using practical examples, Arthur and Mike clearly illustrate that Customer Service does not have to be an oxymoron."
Henry Barenblatt, CEO, Research Surveys (Pty) Ltd.

"At last – a readable, understandable, no nonsense, plain English approach to Customer Service as it has never been told before."
Denis Kaye, Chairman, Stuttafords Van Lines

"Prescribed reading for all South Africans; mandatory for those in the service industry."
Anton Thompson, Chairman, Thompson's Tours

"A highly motivational and practical guide for getting and staying close to your Customers. Juiced! is one of the best books on Customer Service I've read."
Reg Lascaris, Co-Chairman, Hunt Lascaris

"Juiced! is easy to read and easy to understand. To those who absorb and evaluate its message, it will have a dramatic impact on their lives and the lives of their Customers."
Val Leech, Sales Development and Training Manager, Tupperware Southern Africa

"This is certainly an extremely informative, enlightening and inspiring book that is most timely. Every South African will benefit greatly from the excellent case studies and the many positive and practical guidelines outlined in an entertaining and easy-to-read manner. I will certainly encourage every one of my students and colleagues to read it."
Professor Ernie Heath, head of Department of Tourism Management and Director of The Centre for Afrika-tourism, University of Pretoria

"This book will certainly challenge each one of us, in an enjoyable, light-hearted but serious way, to assess our stand on providing service. It is short, sharp, practical and filled with ideas and case studies."
Peter Quinn, Managing Director, The Fedics Group Ltd.

"It was a pleasure to read a book on Customer Service written by South Africans in a language and style that South Africans can relate to. A great book for any business."
Enver Asmal, Managing Director, Profour Projects

"Your book energised me and left me feeling upbeat – it's like a vitamin B injection for the brain! Well done, Arthur and Mike."
Brett Gage, Chief Executive Officer, Clarins SA

"This book illustrates that Customer Service is about attitude, not money, and gives easy steps and tips to transform yourself and your business. Mike and Arthur show that South African service can be world class."
Steve Griessel, Executive Chairman, Tourvest

"The book exudes the enthusiasm for the service that it preaches."
Jaco Levenink, Die Burger

"If Juiced! jumpstarts even a small current through the veins of South Africans, it will translate to instant prosperity. I'd go as far as saying that Juiced! should be piped through our water system. Good service is, after all, a matter of national health."
Les Aupias, Carte Blanche

"Juiced! galvanises a collective positive mindset for engendering a successful Customer relationship through a conscious culture of humanity, passion and dedication."
Derek Thema, Tribute Magazine

"This book provides valuable insight into the extraordinary business of achieving your Customer Service goals"
Jacques Kempen, CEO, Rebhold Ltd

"This is a stunning piece of work. If we care enough about our staff, colleagues and especially our clients, then this book is the perfect gift for each of them. Light-hearted yet full of energy and voema."
Graham Power, CEO, Power Group of Companies

"Certainly, if we could manage to put into practise one comment a day, 95% of foreign visitors would return as friends. A book well worth the pause in a busy schedule!"
Francois Rogers, Director: Office of the Minister of Environmental Affairs and Tourism

"Taken seriously, this book will assist all those who read it to achieve their goals and dreams."
Keith Kirsten, CEO, Keith Kirsten Horticulture International

"This book just oozes passion and creative advice on excellence in service. It provides outstanding guidelines on leadership, focus and implementation."
Errol Stern, Managing Director, USABCO (Pty) Ltd

"Arthur's and Mike's passion for service excellence has finally bubbled over, and the result is an exhilarating read! Buy this book, read it and implement it – this is your contribution towards South Africa becoming a winning nation!"
Otto J Stehlik, Executive Chairman, Protea Hospitality Corporation

"Get Juiced with yet another business read from Mike Lipkin and Arthur Gillis. It's full of the Power and Passion of previous books and right up there with what the 'new economy' now needs. . . Spectacular Customer Service. If you want to give your company some extra power then step on the Juice with Mike and Arthur."
John Barton, Deputy CEO, Mondi Paper

Juiced!

How To Succeed Through Spectacular Customer Service

Arthur Gillis Mike Lipkin

Copyright 2000 by Arthur Gillis and Mike Lipkin
First edition in 2000 by Touch The Sky Publishers
16 Castle Street, Fellside, Johannesburg 2192
Cover photograph by Peter Baasch
Reproduction by KCB Typesetting
Printed and bound by Supreme Printers

"No pessimist ever discovered the secrets of the stars, or sailed to an uncharted land, or opened a new heaven to the human spirit."

Helen Keller

"We dedicate this book to all the optimists in this country who see what it can be, not what it can't."

Arthur Gillis and Mike Lipkin

"God doesn't make orange juice; God makes oranges."

Jesse Jackson

Welcome to Juiced.co.za!

Juiced: *filled with power, vitality, commitment, energy; really turned on and fired up; unstoppable and irresistible*

We know you're running so hard, you hardly have time to catch your breath. That's why this book is for people who don't have time to read books. It's been designed to help you "get it" immediately. Because if you don't get it immediately, how can we get you Juiced? Think of this book as nutritious, fun, fat-free, fast food for your brain.

We've pumped all our experience and energy into Juiced! We've taken Arthur's lessons from the hotel business, the ultimate 24/7/365 industry and blended it with Mike's sales and motivation expertise. After all, aren't we all really in the business of hosting people while selling and motivating them?

Yes, this is a book on Customer Service. But think about it: isn't everyone in your life your Customer? Some are Customers of the non-paying kind, but every relationship you have is based on some kind of exchange – love, money, favours, trust, faith. So Customer Service is not just an act. It's a way of life. It's an attitude. It's about making a difference. It's about making people happy. It's about being Juiced because you're chasing a dream or connecting deeply with another person.

Hey, here's the **BIG** question: when are you truly at your finest? Isn't it when you're serving someone else motivated mainly by their wellbeing? Isn't when you're helping someone who you care more about than yourself? Aren't you at your best when you're giving generously and gracefully?

Yes, we hear you say, but WHAT ABOUT THE MONEY? WHAT ABOUT THE SUCCESS YOU PROMISED US ON THE FRONT COVER? Well, that's the whole point of getting Juiced! If you practise the simple principles we share with you on the following pages, you will be more successful than you can ever imagine. Here's the main insight, though, and this is what "Juiced!" is all about:

You will only be successful if you make others successful. If you only do it so you can become successful, you will fail.

This is a book for people who know that all they'll ever need, they have within themselves right now. It doesn't matter whether you're a CEO or a cashier. What matters is that you really, really want to be the most You that You can be.

Give us just a few hours of your time, and we'll make you massively successful by giving you the tools, insights, principles and stories of some of the world's finest Customer Service Champions. Everything you read in Juiced! has been inspired by the thousands of outstanding people with whom we've had the privilege of working.

Everything you read about in Juiced! is fresh. This book is made up of our "newest and most improved" ingredients. What's more, although we both have wide international exposure, some of the people who've inspired us most are South Africans. Contrary to popular belief, we believe that Customer Service in South Africa is good and it's getting better. Read on to find out more.

Enjoy getting Juiced! And please, let us know what you think by visiting www.mikelipkin.com and leaving a message, or by faxing us on (011) 728-6907. What's more, if you've got any great examples of Spectacular Customer Service, send them to us. If we publish them, we'll give you full credit.

A few thanks before we get started

We'd like to thank the CNA for making this book possible. It was only on the strength of their commitment to helping us make Juiced! a best-seller that we could proceed.

For their invaluable input, we thank Ronnie Apteker, Henry Barenblatt, Danny Bryer, Bernard Cassar, Arnold Cloete, Ruth Davies, Peter de Klerk, Allan Duke, William Ford, Barry Gerson, Gordon Joffe, Philip Krawitz, Reg Lascaris, Miso Markovina, Mary McGuire, Eric Molobi, Jimmy Ntintili, Carol Scott, Aart van der Heijden, Gary Walker, Barbara Wilson, the special staff of Protea Hotels and all the extraordinary people and companies who appear on the following pages.

A special thanks also goes to Otto Stehlik who, as one of the true Customer Service visionaries, has inspired thousands of people to have faith and belief in themselves.

We're also grateful to Terry Lamb from Supreme Printers who once again helped produce a superb product in record time.

Of course, nothing could have happened without the love and support of our families – Ashli, Anton, Alexis and Annette Gillis and Dani-Emma, Carla, Anthony and Hilary Lipkin.

And finally, we thank you for investing in Juiced! and making all our efforts pay off. Viva, all our readers, Viva!

How to use this book to get Juiced!

You decide. There are many ways to use this book. Here are a few that may interest you: the first is simply to read it, enjoy it and apply it where appropriate.

The second way is to only read the Non-Readers Summary. Instead of a mere Contents page, over the next sixteen pages you will find the key highlights of the book. If you just read the summary, you'll take away all of the main points. If you want to dig deeper, then simply turn to the page indicated next to the particular highlight that interests you.

The third way is to get everyone around you Juiced by sharing the book. We'd prefer that you didn't photocopy the pages, so you may wish to invest in a few copies for your colleagues and Customers. (We're just grabbing a quick opportunity to help you by selling you some more books!) Then choose a particular point that is relevant to your challenges, request that your stakeholders read it, and then workshop it in your company. You may even wish to invite Mike or Arthur to facilitate the session for you.

A unique special offer and a publishing first: If you fax us proof that you have invested in ten or more copies of **Juiced**! from the CNA, we'll send you a free 60 minute motivational video which normally retails for R395. Simply fax the sales slip and your postal address to (011) 728-6907.

The Non-Readers Summary of Juiced!

why you're doing what you're doing. A little Reward and Recognition will also get your motor running, but you have to know how you're doing. 57-58

It's not good enough being a leader, you have to be a cheerleader. Become famous for your enthusiasm. If you show that you cannot handle the stress, or if you demonstrate your anxiety, your colleagues' and Customers' morale will crumble like puff pastry. 59-60

Here are Seven unquestionable truths of great Cheer-leaders: 60

The marketplace is not a charity organization: you have to be strong for others. 60-61

Win your own Academy Award. If you act the part, you'll get the role. 61-62

Above all else, your colleagues and Customers want you to take away their psychological insecurity. No matter how old we become, there's a part of us that will always be five years old. Neglect the emotions of the people around you, and you will perish. 62-63

How are you helping people cope with the Five Deadly South African Plagues: murder, rape, theft, fire and floods? 63-65

Do you lead by example? Are you one of the few who *do* versus the many who *talk?* When our actions are not consistent with our beliefs, we become frustrated, angry and depressed. 65-66

Become famous for your enthusiasm. One of the rarest sights in South Africa today is a genuinely happy person who genuinely loves serving her Customers. If

If it's delivered more than 24 hours after the event, the feedback has exceeded its use-by-date. Burn the annual review. 210-211

Prescription without diagnosis is malpractice. If you keep asking the right questions, your staff members will give themselves the right answers. 211-212

Our final words and a final request: be a resource not just a resident. Be a participant not a passenger. And be Juiced not jaded. The two sweetest sounding words in the English language are "Thank you". 213

Part One

Hey, Gillis and Lipkin, what the heck is this thing called *Spectacular Customer Service?*

"Simple, do the basics right consistently and add a Little Extra Touch. In fact, don't even worry about the Extra Touch. Just get the basics right consistently."

Spectacular Customer Service is not about renting helicopters in snowstorms to get the parcel delivered on time. It is not about spending thousands of Rands on Customers so that they feel important. It's not about calling on your people to perform acts of heroism and self-sacrifice under fire. And it's not about complex service models that impress the stupid and confuse the staff.

Spectacular Customer Service simply means making sure that results match Customer's expectations. If this is all you do, you will be massively successful. If you take it up a tiny notch and go just one step beyond matching expectations, you and your company will be untouchable. But this is not as easy as it sounds. You know why? Because Customers' expectations are growing daily. The Internet, the global economy, saturated markets, fierce competition, growing income and education levels, the media, higher personal standards and time pressures are all converging to raise the bar dramatically for Customer Service providers.

Customer Service is first and foremost the management of promises. Practise the Japanese principle of Maykoto and you don't have to read any further than this point.

"The number one affliction of today's adults is disillusionment."

Ally McBeal

Isn't Customer Service really just the management of promises? If you keep every promise you ever make to a Customer, isn't that really Spectacular Customer Service? That's why the Japanese believe that Maykoto is the highest form of quality. It means simply: say what you're going to do and then go out and do it.

However, dear fellow Customer Service Provider, how many times have you made promises that you didn't keep? How many people have you let down in your life? How many times have other people disappointed you in your life? If you think about it, aren't the most painful moments in your life those times when you've been let down by others, especially those who you trusted to come through for you?

You know what? Most of us have been let down so many times that we've become cynical. We're almost afraid to get too excited about anything because we don't want to be disappointed again. So be very careful about what you promise others. It's easy to promise the world. Those glossy brochures offering us paradise and riches have suckered us all. We've all been the victims of fast-talking salespeople and slick advertising campaigns. But the people who simply always honour their promises are the people who will be successful in the long run. Are you one of them? If you are, you don't really need to read any further. Just keep doing what you're doing consistently. You're welcome to stay with us, of course. But this book is really for the rest of you, ordinary people like us, being called on to keep extraordinary promises in extremely difficult times. We promise you'll really enjoy what you're about to read.

You have to really, really, really love helping people. You have to love them at their best and at their baddest, when they're silent or when they're shouting, whether they're sixteen or septuagenarian, pink or purple. Be an Amateur: do it for the love and the money will follow.

"The major reason capable people fail to advance is that they don't work well with their colleagues and Customers. The statement, 'He's good, but he has trouble getting along with other people,' is the kiss of death for management potential. . .The key to success is not information. It's people." *Lee Iacocca*

Here's the most important Customer Service question you will ever be asked:

How well do you handle difficult people?

Do you respond to them with grace? Can they feel how much you want to help them even if they're super-uptight? Do you love the game called Customer Service even when it becomes rough, tough and enough? Do you love helping people just for the sake of it?

At the start of our time together, we can tell you this truth: Spectacular Customer Service is never about money. It's always about making other people feel good. We often joke in our seminars that we aren't doing it for the money. We quickly add that we'll take the Customer's money because we have certain overheads, but that's not the real motivation for doing what we're doing. It's true. If you're just doing it for the bucks, you'll burn out. We guarantee it. But if you're doing it because you are Juiced by adding value to the people around you, you'll keep growing and becoming more successful. We base this statement on the thousands of highly successful people with whom we work every year. The great ones stay inspired year after year after year. The rest are fly-by-nighters. They succeed for a month or a year or even two before falling by the wayside because they have nothing to sustain them in the tough times.

In order to make the South African Olympic Team, you have to meet the qualifying standard. Well, we're all Olympic Athletes and we all have to make the team. In Customer Service, Customer Expectations are the Qualifying Standard. Have you met them?

If you're in Customer Service, you're an athlete. You have to run faster, jump higher and be stronger. You have to know how to keep swimming when you're in over your head. You have to dive in head first. You have to bend over backwards. You have to have massive stamina, especially in the closing stages of any event. You have to consistently train yourself to stay in peak condition. Your ultimate goal is always the Gold Medal. And the judges are always the Customers.

So what do Customers expect from you? What's the qualifying standard in your industry? How do the best of the best perform in your market? How do you rate? Are you the current Gold Medal Holder? Silver? Bronze? Have you even made it to the finals? Or are you bringing up the rear?

Our hunch, is that if you're reading this book, you're at least among the medallists. The non-qualifiers wouldn't even have bothered to pick it up. Their response would be the classic Losers' Chant: "What for? There's nothing I can learn from those guys. I know what I've got to do. I've got better things to do with my time."

Seriously, have you met the Qualifying Standard? Do you even know what it is? Many of the companies with whom we work struggle to describe the Qualifying Standard. As a result, they struggle to match Customer expectations. If you were standing in front of us right now and we asked you: what are the precise expectations that your Customers and Prospects have of you versus your competition, what would your answer be? Could you tell us quickly and fluently? Or would you battle to give us a clear answer?

Can we make a suggestion? Do not proceed until you've thought deeply about these questions: What is the qualifying standard of your industry? Do you meet it? Why? Do you exceed it? How? And most importantly, do you meet and exceed the Qualifying Standard consistently? Are you Juiced?

Anyone can have an Excellent Game, but only the best have Game Excellence *(Anthony Robbins).* **Consistency is the Holy Grail of Customer Service. Whoever is most consistent wins.**

It's not good enough just making the Qualifying Standard some of the time. You have to make it all of the time. That's the mark of Spectacular Service. Anyone can have a good day once or even twice a week. The champions have a great day seven days a week. You know why? Because they know they have no alternative. They have a down day on their own time. But when they're getting paid to serve someone, they burn their excuses. They raise their game and hit the Qualifying Standard. Do you?

Remember this ultimate Customer Service truth: whoever is most consistent wins. Consistency is the Holy Grail of Customer Service. You know why? Because Customers have extremely short memories. We're all only as good as our last act of Customer Service. One shocking experience can wipe out the Goodwill Bank of all the previous favourable experiences.

Consistency also applies to all the people in your organization. It can take you a lifetime to build a reputation for quality and consistency. It can take just one rude employee to bring it all crashing down in a moment. So look around you. Your personal success is dependent on each and every one of your colleagues. An injury to one Customer is an injury to all the people in the company serving that Customer.

So the next time you see a fellow colleague not delivering Spectacular Customer Service, step up and step in. Coach your colleague. Take responsibility. If that Customer walks away upset, your wellbeing is in danger. It doesn't matter who saw it happen. What matters is that you've allowed someone to leave your business not as a fan but as a foe. And that's the kiss of Customer Service death.

Here are some examples of Qualifying Standards in different service industries. These examples are based on our point of view only. Feel free to disagree. We don't mind. Decide for yourself and add your own.

If you are in the *Hotel* business, we believe your coffee must be freshly brewed and hot. Your beds and pillows must be firm. The linen must be freshly laundered and fresh. The staff must be courteous and the rooms spotless.

If you are in the *Motivation, Service and Sales Training* business, you need to entertain and inform your Delegates while giving them practical take-home tools that they can immediately apply to their profit.

If you are in the *Restaurant* business, the atmosphere must relax your Guests. The food must be superior to the food they would have at home and the pace of service should just exceed their patience.

If you are in the *Car Rental* business, the right car must be there at the right time and it must be clean. You must get the Customer into the car quickly. The tank must be full and everything must work.

If you are in the *Banking* business, you must manage Customers' money with accuracy, consistency and provide maximum security. There must be no surprises.

If you are in the *Hospital* business, you must do all you can to heal your Patients in the time that you said you would while minimizing their discomfort and pain.

If you are in the *Retail* business, you must offer your Customers the right merchandise at the right price in an environment that makes them want to stay longer.

If you're in the *TV or Movie* business, you must remove Viewers from reality for 1-3 hours by making them laugh, cry, shout, gasp, sigh, relax or celebrate.

If you're in the *IT* business, you must give Customers exactly what you promised in the time that you promised. And the end result must be a quicker, more effective system than the preceding one.

Finally, *we believe that if you're in any kind of service business, you're really in the business of making your Customers' lives better because of your intervention.* Everything you do must increase their wellbeing – from the first contact to the final delivery. This includes: prompt return of phone calls, product knowledge, integrity, commitment, courtesy, efficiency, thoroughness, professionalism, caring, respect and keeping promises.

Yup, it's an awesome achievement even getting the basics right. Don't worry, though, we'll give you a formula for meeting and even exceeding the Qualifying Standards.

Now let's look at how the Gold Medallists exceed the Qualifying Standard by adding the Little Extra Touch.

We have chosen eighteen Customer Service Champions who, based on our combined experience and opinion, are among the best in the world. Some are massive companies and some are micro. Some are individual people and one is even a canine. The bottom line is that they all raised their standard beyond the Qualifying Standard to the satisfaction and delight of their Customers.

Amazon.com.

Have you ever visited Amazon? Click onto their Website right now: www.amazon.com. Spend some time there. Browse around their offerings. We believe Amazon is one of the benchmarks of Spectacular Customer Service in the e-economy.

In the December 27 1999 issue of Time Magazine, the founder of Amazon, Jeff Bezos, was reported as saying, "Our vision is to be the world's most Customer-centric company. The place where people come to find and discover anything they might want to buy online." The article goes on to talk about the "Six Core Values" of the company:

Customer Obsession
Ownership
Bias For Action
Frugality
High Hiring Bar
Innovation

The vision and core values are featured on billboard size banners that "festoon the aisles and walls" of the Amazon offices and warehouses. The article goes on to describe Bezos's philosophy, "His *Six Core Value* speech is the linchpin of most of his speaking engagements. He always begins with the watchword of his faith: the Customer comes first. "Wake up every morning terrified – not of the competition but of our Customers."

Our personal experience with Amazon reinforces these words. Whenever we click on the site, we are greeted by these words, "Welcome back, Mr Mike Lipkin", or "Welcome back, Mr Gillis." In fact, Mike is a frequent buyer of books through Amazon. Recently, he spent a month overseas and didn't visit Amazon for four weeks. Here is the e-mail he received in the fifth week after his last purchase:

> *"We noticed that you haven't shopped with us in a while and we thought we might be able to help you discover your next great book or CD.*
>
> *One of the best ways to find a new favourite is to see what other people are enjoying. At Amazon, we've used our large community of over 10 million Customers to create the Amazon.com Hot 100 lists of our best-selling book and music titles. These lists are updated regularly and feature titles priced at our everyday savings of up to 40% off.*
>
> *We've included the top five titles from each list for your browsing pleasure below. (At least, these were the top five as of when we sent this message)."*

This kind of letter and the personal greeting every time we visit their Website is why we believe Amazon is a Gold Medallist. Amazon treat us with more warmth and recognition than most human beings we deal with. By the way, how do you wake up your Customers who've gone quiet on you?

Seekers Travel.

Mike used to use a different travel agency to do his air-travel bookings. Seekers found a way to save him almost 50% on domestic flights through clever packages and deals. When he went back to his previous agency, they couldn't tell him why they couldn't match these prices. In one year, Seekers saved Mike over R50 000. More than just a Little Extra Touch, we would say. We would also add that the travel agency that Mike used previously is a big national operation. It just shows you, even in a commodity type industry, the Gold Medallists can set themselves apart very effectively.

Wagamama's Japanese Restaurant in Sandton City.

Yes, the food is good at Wagamama's. And yes, the atmosphere and service meet the Qualifying Standard. But what wins Wagamama's the Little Extra Touch Award is the massage you're given while you wait for your meal. Wagamama's has invested in an extra staff member who roves the restaurant with a three-balled Japanese massage instrument. When she sees a Customer looking a little hassled or impatient, she offers him a massage. Of course, he loves it and the whole table demands a chance. It's the topic of conversation for the next fifteen minutes.

Fortune and Fast Company Magazines.

In writing this book, we researched Spectacular Service providers and stories from around the world. Obviously we clicked onto the Fortune Website. As one of the world's leading business magazines, we knew we would find some rich information there. And we did. The Fortune online archives on Customer Service were fascinating and comprehensive. However, when we clicked onto the Business Week Website, we were informed that only Subscribers had access to their database. We didn't have a password, so we were denied access.

Fast Company, on the other hand, is a hot new business magazine that is just four years old. It has been called "Fortune on steroids." It has an outstanding Website where you can get the entire current issue of the magazine online. They hold nothing back. A rival magazine, Success, only features part of their articles online. For the rest, you have to buy the magazine. Well, we certainly won't.

Both Fortune and Fast Company win the Little Extra Touch Award by showing that it always pays to be generous to both Customers and Prospects.

Imperial Car Rental and Budget Rent a Car.

On a recent trip to Richards Bay, Mike arrived at the Airport at 14h00 in 40-degree heat with a 100% humidity factor. It was like walking through soup. Mike was carrying his materials and bags and, within seconds, was sweating profusely. Coming from the dry air of Johannesburg and not being used to this, he craved a drink as he approached the car he had rented through Imperial. Lo and behold, as he entered his vehicle, two things massively increased his wellbeing. Firstly, the car was already cool because the air-conditioning was already on. And, even more impressively, there was an ice-cold can of Coca-Cola placed in the holder between the front seats.

The next day at his public seminar, Mike asked an Imperial manager whether it was Imperial policy to place cold drinks in cars on hot days. She replied that it was not. When Mike told her about the Coke in the car the afternoon before, the manager smiled and told Mike that the Coke was the idea of the young woman who managed the afternoon shift. Purely on her own initiative, she went to the kiosk in the airport building and bought four Cokes out of petty cash. Then, as she saw the baggage coming off the plane, she ran to the four cars and placed a cold drink in each one of them. Clearly, she delivered a world class Little Extra Touch.

Arthur uses Budget Rent a Car. The Little Extra Touch that motivates him to give them his loyalty is the trolley that they bring to his car every time he enters the parking lot to return the vehicle. They know that he always has luggage and so they bring him the trolley in anticipation of his needs. What's more they greet him by name and are genuinely grateful for his business.

The World Championship of Customer Service: South Africa versus America.

There is another reason why we have included Budget Car Rental here. In December 1999, Mike visited America where he rented a car from Hertz. A week before Christmas, a tyre blew just outside a really small town called Stroudsburg in Pennsylvania. It was ten o'clock at night, it was below zero and Mike was with his family, stranded in the middle of nowhere. The car was a Ford Explorer and Mike didn't have a clue how to change the tyre. He couldn't even find the spare which, he discovered later, was stored underneath the car. His only lifeline was the phone number on the tag attached to the car keys.

Fortunately, the Lipkins got stuck about half a mile from the nearest store. They walked there and called the number listed on the tag. A woman took Mike's details and asked him to wait at the store. Within 30 minutes two men in a tow-truck had arrived. They took the keys from Mike, changed the tyre and were back within fifteen minutes. Then they gave the Lipkins a lift back to the car and left. Total time elapsed from Mike's call to a central office to the resolution of the problem: 45 minutes. Mike was blown away. He told Arthur that he doubted a South African company could offer service of that calibre.

As usual, Arthur took up the challenge. He called Budget and told them that he was in a car rented from them. He told them he was stuck just outside Colesberg, a small town in the Karoo even smaller than Stroudsburg. He said that he had a puncture and he was having difficulty removing the wheel nuts. Marion from Budget apologized profusely for the inconvenience. She said that someone would be dispatched from Colesberg and would be on the scene within fifteen minutes – an even better performance than Hertz delivered to Mike in America. Who said South African companies can't take on the world's best companies and win?

The Youthful Breakfast Team at the Protea Hotel President in Cape Town.

Do yourself a favour. If you want to see enthusiasm in action, go and have breakfast at the Protea Hotel President in Seapoint, Cape Town. We're not telling you to do this for the food. It's good.

We're not even telling to go there for the view, which is brilliant. We're telling you to go there for the young staff who'll serve you. They are mostly students who are embarking on a career in the hospitality industry. There is a spring in their step. They are anxious to do the right thing. They are excited about what they do and their excitement is contagious. Their attitude will shower you with a series of Little Extra Touches. If you've ever doubted whether you should give a young person a chance, even if they don't have the qualifications or the experience, go to the Protea Hotel President for breakfast. You won't just get fed, you'll get Juiced!

The Young Counter Staff at Seattle Coffee in Hyde Park and Killarney, Johannesburg.

Seattle Coffee is a new chain of coffee bars in Johannesburg and Cape Town. It's designed along the same lines as Starbucks in North America. The décor is exquisite and the coffee is good, but the real reason to go there is the young, trendy staff behind the counter. It's a Little Extra Touch all on its own to watch them work with each other, especially in peak trading periods. Their energy and camaraderie permeate the shop. Once again, another reason to give youth a chance.

A quick aside: the Spectacular Customer Service Paradox(1) as revealed by the youth at the Protea Hotel President and Seattle Coffee.

Here is the paradox of many Customer Service providers: the newer and more inexperienced they are, the higher their motivation levels, the greater their willingness to go the extra inch. They tend to be more energetic, optimistic and resourceful.

Then, the longer they serve Customers, the more cynical and fatigued they become. They discover just how tough it is to keep pleasing people who are not pleased. They find out just how much of a toll it takes to stay cheerful in a cheerless environment. They run out of energy and then they run out of passion.

All of us in Customer Service have one massive challenge: how do we preserve the naive love we had for Customers when we were young, as we grow older?

The Ritz Carlton Hotel in St Louis, Missouri, USA.

The Ritz Carlton is a well-respected chain of 5-star hotels across North America. However, the reason why we include them here is a charming Little Extra Touch that is unique to the Ritz Carlton. It's so small and yet so meaningful that we can't understand why no one else in the world does it. And the beauty is that it costs almost nothing.

Here's what happened: we were sitting at the bar in the lobby of the hotel having a pre-dinner drink when Mike had to go to the bathroom. He didn't know where it was so he asked the waitress to direct him. Instead of just pointing in the general direction, she actually walked Mike all the way to the facility. And this was despite the fact that it was Happy Hour and she was under considerable pressure to serve a mass of Customers. When Mike told Arthur about this Little Extra Touch, Arthur said that it was service policy at all Ritz Carlton Hotels to actually walk Guests to their desired destination. It's a small gesture that makes a big difference. Try it in your business today.

Cape Union Mart.

This is a group of 20 stores distributed throughout South Africa which specializes in outdoor and leisure clothing, equipment and footwear. They call themselves "Pioneers in Outdoor Adventure" and they really walk their talk. Whatever you want for your outdoor adventure, you'll find it there. They also have a very Customer-friendly price and return policy: firstly, they guarantee that they'll match anyone's price anywhere; secondly, if the item you purchased goes on sale within 30 days, you will be refunded the difference in price; thirdly, they guarantee everything they sell. So, if your item doesn't stand the test of "fair wear and tear," it will be replaced. Finally, when you buy an item from the store, you are advised by staff to keep it in its wrapping until you use it. The reason is that if you don't use the item within twelve months of purchase, Cape Union Mart will give you a full refund.

The real reason, though, why we've included Cape Union Mart in our list of Gold Medallists is their staff. When you enter a Cape Union Mart store, the staff greet you with warmth, they are helpful without being pushy and they are extremely knowledgeable, not only about their merchandise but about what you'll need for your outdoor adventure.

Part of the reason why you'll find such great service in a Cape Union Mart store is the passion for service of Philip Krawitz, the CEO. For example, Philip has coached his staff never to say, "Can I help you?" to Customers because the answer invariably is, "No, just browsing." This is one of the biggest mistakes many retail staff make. They invite a negative response before they've even got to know what the Customer wants. If you're involved in retailing, please take this lesson to heart. However, at Cape Union Mart, when a

Customer touches the merchandise, it's a non-verbal request for information. Then the staff member will explain the virtues of the product to the Customer.

In an amusing aside, Philip shared the story about one of his manageresses with us. This was a woman who had to deal with Customers at a very high level, so Philip sent her on a course designed to help her conduct herself appropriately at business and social functions. On her return, she told Philip that she now knew what culture really meant. Culture, she said, meant "getting out of a motorcar with both knees together." Like Philip, if you can laugh with your staff, your Customers will do the same.

Nordstrom, USA.

Whenever we go the USA, we make a point of visiting Nordstrom, a chain of clothing stores widely acknowledged to be America's Number One Service Company. We always buy a shirt or a tie just for the opportunity to interact with the Nordstrom sales staff. They are extraordinary. Their job consists almost entirely of delivering a constant stream of Little Extra Touches. Working at Nordstrom is not for everybody. Demands and expectations are high. It's tough to get in. Income is comprised mostly of commission on sales so salespeople are really motivated to perform, but the pressure is relentless. Nordstrom salespeople are more than just salespeople, they are fashion consultants. Customers come to them for advice on clothes as much as they do for the clothes themselves.

When employees start work at Nordstrom, they are given a little one-sided card instead of a handbook. This is what it says:

WELCOME TO NORDSTROM

We're glad to have you with our company.
Our number one goal is to provide outstanding Customer Service.
Set both your personal and professional goals high.

We have great confidence in your ability to achieve them.
Nordstrom Rules:
Rule #1: Use your good judgement in all situations.
There will be no additional rules.
Please feel free to ask your department manager, store manager, or divisional general manager any question at any time.

Now we know what you're thinking. It requires high quality salespeople to handle that kind of freedom to make decisions. Well, those kind of people are in massive supply in South Africa. Both of us give that kind of freedom to the people around us and they almost always rise to the challenge.

Finally, Nordstrom expects, encourages, preaches, and demands individual initiative and ideas from its frontline people. Their evaluations and income depend on it. How much effort are you investing in squeezing that kind of Juice out of your own people and yourself as well?

Thabo Mbeki and Trevor Manuel.

Both Mbeki and Manuel win the Gold Medallist Award for their service to South Africa. They have steered the economy safely through a rough passage. Manuel has won many plaudits from the private sector, while Mbeki has established a reputation as a "strong, firm, decisive, articulate leader in control." (Financial Mail March 24 2000) Both of them have demonstrated extraordinary grace under pressure. They have held their ground and been utterly consistent. Both of them have so far exceeded the Qualifying Standard.

Bob Skinstad.

Arthur's youngest daughter, Alexis, once ran onto the field for the Stormers Rugby Team as a mascot. A few weeks later, Arthur sat next to Bob Skinstad, a member of the Stormers team, on a flight from Johannesburg to Cape Town. Arthur told Bob how thrilled his daughter was to be given that honour. Bob asked Arthur how old Alexis was. Arthur told him that she was about to have her Batmitzvah – she was turning twelve a month later. Well, a week before the event, Bob faxed a personal message of goodwill to her. Alexis was so thrilled that she read out the message at her party.

We believe that Little Extra Touch by Bob went way above and beyond the call of duty of a sports celebrity. That's why Bob will do well in whatever he decides to do. He is motivated by genuine goodwill and he is making a lot of friends as he goes along – including a little twelve year old girl called Alexis.

By the way, Bob understands that if you do something special for someone's spouse or children, they will love you forever. We all want what is best for our loved ones and anyone who can help give us that will have our undying loyalty.

Jimmy Ntintili.

Jimmy Ntintili is an extraordinary entrepreneur who pioneered packaged tours into South Africa's townships. Today, he not only has a thriving business, but he invests major amounts of his time in helping other fledging tour companies learn to fly. He is a gifted storyteller, art collector, raconteur and businessperson.

We wanted Jimmy's input into this book because we believe he is Juiced! Like many other highly successful people, Jimmy's diary was crammed with business and social commitments. He just couldn't see us during the day. So he asked us to come to his house at night where he told us his service philosophy over a bottle of excellent chilled Chardonnay. We spent three hours with him and we learnt the meaning of true hospitality – not just of his home and drink but of his mind and soul. Here's to you, Jimmy Ntintili!

Mel Gibson.

What has Mel Gibson got to do with Spectacular Customer Service, we hear you asking. Simply this: Mel's Qualifying Standard is that he must meet our expectations of an exciting movie every time we lay out our hard-earned cash for a cinema ticket. We want to forget our troubles by escaping into another world far away, where we can let Mel take control of our lives for a couple of hours. And Mel always comes through. He is remarkably consistent. In Braveheart, Ransom, Payback, Mad Max, Lethal Weapon 1,2,3 & 4, Gibson delivers – unlike most of his Hollywood counterparts.

Toby, the 3-year old cross between a Staffordshire Terrier and a Maltese Poodle.

From Mel Gibson to a streetbreed canine – you must admit we're rolling out an unlikely cast of Customer Service Gold Medallists. But what do we really want from others? Well, the ideal companion or colleague would be unfailingly loyal. She would always be ecstatic to see us. She would never be in a bad mood. She would always be there for us in the tough moments. She would express her affection openly and unreservedly. She would act with world-class consistency. She would have the heart of a lion and go after anything that threatened the wellbeing of her team. She would always act with the best interests of the team in mind. She would never carry a grudge, take rejection personally or lie. She would be a great listener and she would love people. She would be slow to anger and immediately forgive others. Oh, by the way, she would also be absolutely gorgeous.

You've just been reading about Mike's dog, Toby, the 3-year old cross between a Staffordshire Terrier and a Maltese Poodle. Toby always meets and exceeds the Qualifying Standard. We can learn from anyone and anything. Your pets may just be the best teachers you have. So reciprocate their unconditional love, loyalty and respect.

L.L. Bean Inc Retail Company, Maine, USA (reported in Fast Company Magazine March 2000).

According to Elizabeth Spaulding, Vice President Customer Satisfaction, the L.L. Bean premise is simple: "If any product doesn't meet a Customer's expectations – whatever they may be – we will replace it, repair it or refund the Customer's money. Today, if a Customer calls and wants to return a Maine Hunting Shoe, the first thing we do is find out what the Customer's expectations were when she bought the shoe. If she expected it to last ten years, then there's no question – we'll replace the shoe. If it turns out that she expected it to last only one year, then we'll repair the shoe. The point is that the Customer determines the expectation, not us."

L.L.Bean's operating philosophy is based on their belief that 99.9% of their Customers are totally honest. But the real reason why we love this company is that their entire policy is driven by the individual expectations of the Customer, not the "returns policy" of the company. How does your company handle returns? Is your approach totally Customer-centric? Or are you force-fitting Customers according to what suits you? George Bernard Shaw said it right when he wrote:

> *"The only man I know who behaves sensibly is my tailor; he takes my measures anew each time he sees me. The rest go on with their old measurements and expect me to fit them."*

Singapore Airlines LTD (reported in Fast Company Magazine March 2000).

Yap Kim Wah, Senior Vice President of Marketing Services for Singapore Airlines, expresses the concept of the Little Extra Touch beautifully when he says, "The most important thing that you can do for Customers is make them feel cared for as individuals. That means doing the little things, looking for opportunities to provide extra Customer care. It means making Passengers feel as if everything you do is especially for them – how you serve a cup of tea, with just the right amount of sugar, or the way you deal with a particular Passenger's plight."

Let us ask you, how cared for do you make your Customers feel? Do they feel that everything you do is designed specifically for them? Or do they feel as though they are clones of every other Customer who ever dealt with you?

Yap Kim Wah goes on to tell a great story of how one of Singapore Airlines' flight attendants applied this Little Extra Touch very resourcefully, "On a recent overseas flight, one of our attendants noticed a toddler who kept dropping his pacifier. Every time he dropped it, he would cry, and either his mother or another Passenger would retrieve the pacifier, or the flight attendant would get it as she walked by. Finally, the attendant picked up the pacifier, attached it to a ribbon, and sewed it to the child's shirt. The child was happy. The mother was happy. And the Passengers nearby gave the attendant a standing ovation for solving the problem so cleverly. That kind of attention makes all the difference in the world."

Let us ask you, when last did you or your company get a standing ovation from your Customers? Ultimately, isn't that what we should all be aspiring to?

Harry Rosen Menswear, Toronto, Canada.

Recently, Mike visited Toronto, Canada where he delivered a motivational session at a major financial services conference. Mike arrived on Wednesday evening and his session was scheduled for the Friday morning. In his hotel room that night, he read the following Harry Rosen advertisement in a local magazine:

> *"As for our service, we think that even the best shops on Saville Row would be impressed. Here's an example: you have a couple of spare hours between meetings, so you decide to do some shopping. Within 20 minutes, one of our sales associates has guided you to your perfect suit. Ten minutes later, you've already been measured for alterations. And, by the time you return to your hotel that evening, you'll find your masterfully tailored suit ready and waiting for you."*

The next morning, Mike decided to put them to the test. He

needed a new suit anyway. So he visited their store. He was served by a very solicitous young man called Mario who wanted to know exactly what Mike's profession was. Specifically, he wanted to know what kind of image Mike wanted to portray. Then he guided Mike to a range of suits that he believed fitted the brief. It turned out that this young man was also part-owner of a franchise, which he operated with his brother. He appeared fascinated by Mike's stories.

The prices were reasonable. Mike selected his suit. Then he was persuaded to "invest" in a shirt and a tie. Mike almost invested in another pair of shoes, but at the last moment declined the opportunity to "complete the picture of absolute authority and success". The measurements were taken and about 30 minutes later, he was out of the store. It was just after 11h00. When Mike returned to his hotel room at 16h30, the suit was in his room, together with the shirt and tie as well as a note personally signed by Mario thanking Mike for his business and inviting him back soon.

The suit fitted perfectly. But, as impressive as the suit, was the way Harry Rosen created and then matched Mike's high expectations. It was a superb example of big promises followed through by thoroughly professional action. And you know what else? No other store can now take the service high-ground. Harry Rosen owns it. It's one of the ways they are differentiating themselves against their competition. Viva, Harry Rosen, Viva.

The Spectacular Customer Service Paradox(2): It's the easiest and the most difficult part of your business to get right. But if your people are not becoming "Juiced!", they're becoming "Juiceless!"

Let's say you're the CEO of a company with two hundred employees in four offices across South Africa. You're not happy with your information management system because you're not getting the necessary data to make fast, informed decisions. You decide to invest in a new system that completely changes the way your company runs.

Do you think this move could cause problems for your people? Is there likely to be a massive upheaval within the company while 200 people learn a whole new way of managing their business? Is it likely to cost you a fortune? Will the overall performance of the business be negatively impacted in the short term? Of course, the answer is "definitely" to all those questions. You're in for a difficult few months. And we all know that, like a builder, whatever your IT vendor tells you the project is going to cost in time and money, you can conservatively double it.

However, let's say that you decide to improve your service to your Customers. Where do you begin? You can't just order people to improve their service. You can't just bring in an outsider and hope that she can magically galvanize your people into action. Maybe you can offer your people more money if they improve their service, but that's likely to be short-lived. What's more, how do you evaluate the improvement in service anyway? The reality is that there's no easy walk to a Spectacular Customer Service culture. Service is directly connected to culture.

If the company's way of doing business is closed, task-oriented mechanical and insular, there's no way Customer Service will improve. You have a major challenge on your hands. You're looking at a six-month to one-year process before you can hope to deliver Spectacular Service.

On the other hand, let's say that you are already running a reasonably successful, happy, friendly company. Of the 200 people in your company, in line with the 80:20 principle, you have about 40 people who are Customer Service Champions. You know you have to raise the bar of the entire company to meet the Qualifying Standard. What do you do and how long will it take? We believe you can begin to rev up your Customer Service engine almost immediately. You may not even know it, but you've probably already walked quite a long way down the Customer Service path already. Now you need to focus specifically on this vital component of your business. You need to get specific about what it is. You need to take charge and get your peoples' motors running. You need to capture their imaginations and light the fires in their hearts. And do you want to know the best thing of all? It's fun. It's easy. It's about celebration, achievement, fulfilment, growth, excitement, contribution, adventure, love, passion, courage, and making a difference.

All of the companies that we've worked with who've decided to focus powerfully on achieving Spectacular Customer Service have reported a massive jump in employee morale and productivity. You know why? Because Customer Service is about people, it's not about machines. It's about spirit, camaraderie, teamwork, togetherness, common purpose and meaning. So let's ask you this: right now, do you have a massive Customer Service initiative going within your company? If you don't, know this: your people are not becoming "Juiced!" They're becoming "Juiceless".

Here are the three most important reasons why Spectacular Customer Service is so vital to you and your business: One, it will make your people and your Customers very, very happy. Two, it will make you lots and lots of money. Three, it will save you lots and lots of money.

If there's one thing we can promise you with absolute certainty, it's that delivering Spectacular Customer Service will make you, your people and your Customers very, very happy. It's been our experience that people who are performing at their best tend to feel very good about themselves and their company. They feel a sense of pride and a strong sense of belonging. It's also self-evident that Customers who are on the receiving end of this kind of service are also likely to feel very good about the company that's serving them. So if happiness is what you're after, Spectacular Customer Service is the way to get there.

Yes, we can hear you say, "I want my people and my Customers to be happy. But happy doesn't pay the rent or satisfy my shareholders." Well, here some indisputable facts: the better your Customer Service, the higher your margins, the greater your repeat business and the more likely they are to spend more money with you. Even the most cost-conscious of Buyers or Consumers will pay a slight premium for Spectacular Service. And that "slight" premium, even if it's 1-2%, could mean a massive jump in profitability.

In an age where time is more precious than money, many Customers will even pay a large premium for Spectacular Service. Spectacular Customer Service is the best immunity against the Discount Disease. Customers know how rare Spectacular Service is, that's why they're willing to pay more for it. Both of us are "time-poor" which means that we never have enough time to do all the things we want to do. That's why we actively seek out the best of the best Customer Service providers. For us, an hour saved is worth big, big bucks.

You know what else? Happy Customers become walking, talking advertisements for you and your company. Every time you make a Customer happy through an act of Spectacular Service, you've just increased your advertising and promotional budget. Happy Customers become Magnets for other Customers to your business. It's called word-of-mouth advertising and it's like pure gold to you.

The Number-One Challenge for almost every single company on earth is to turn a one-time Customer transaction into a life-time Customer relationship.

We've told you why Spectacular Customer Service will make

your people happy, we've told you why it will make you lots and lots of money. Now let's look at why it will save you lots and lots of money. Did you know that it is six times more expensive to get a new Customer to buy from you than it is for an existing one? That's because you've already done all the hard work. You've attracted the Customer to your business against blistering opposition. You've got to know her and she's got to know you. You've both climbed the learning curve together. You've both got comfortable with each other. You've both got enough change in your life as it is. So both of you want the relationship to work. Positive momentum is on your side. You're swimming with the current. You're feeding off your upfront investment and building on it all the time. You've also done your Customer a massive favour: you've just simplified her life. You've eliminated one more decision that she has to make. She loves you for it. You've turned a one-time transaction into a lifetime relationship – as long as you keep delivering Spectacular Customer Service.

Turned-on people also tend to make fewer mistakes than turned-off people do. So there's far less expense associated with fixing screw-ups that should never have happened in the first place. There are far more "get-it-right-first-times" when turned-on people are driving the company. The operational efficiency rating soars and so does the productivity.

Juiced people also tend to care more about their organizations. They treat their company's assets like their own. Negligence, wastage and shrinkage are all reduced.

Juiced people have personal standards that are higher than the Qualifying Standards, so they raise the overall standards without any pushing from management. In fact, we guarantee you that if you invest strongly in achieving Spectacular Customer Service, your people will keep coming to you with new ideas and initiatives.

Let's move on. If you're not sold by now on the power of

Spectacular Customer Service, you never will be. And, by the way, here's a little insight we'd like to share with you. There are three kinds of people in the world: those who get it, those who are about to get it and those who will never get it. If you are with someone who will never get it, walk away. Don't waste any more of your energy or oxygen. Listen carefully to your sixth sense, your intuition. It will tell you what to do. Remember, if you find yourself arguing with a fool, make sure he isn't doing exactly the same thing.

The Seven Vital Questions your Customers ask themselves before they buy into you.

Just like you, your Customers have Seven Vital Questions that they ask themselves either consciously or subconsciously before they buy. These questions will determine whether they associate with you or not. As you go through these questions, ask yourself how Customers would respond to them when it comes to dealing with you. Would they be Juiced? Rate yourself on each question. They are determining your future:

1. *Do you really have my best interests in mind?*
2. *Can I really trust you?*
3. *What's in it for me?*
4. *What do I have to give up to buy from you?*
5. *What's the risk to me if I make the wrong decision?*
6. *What will other people think of me if I buy from you?*
7. *What should I do?*

Part Two

The Gillis-Lipkin Formula for Spectacular Customer Service.

Make it easy, easy, easy for your Customers to do business with you. And remember: if the game changes, change the gameplan.

Okay, we've told you what Spectacular Customer Service is. We've told you why it's good for you. Now we'll show you how to create it. The entire formula, however, is dependent on one core-bonding agent. Without this factor, the formula will not hold together: *Make it easy, easy, easy for your Customers to do business with you.*

Both of us believe that we have enough mental horsepower to handle all the challenges in front of us. We believe that we're committed to producing quality. We both love dealing with people. We both invest a huge amount of effort in conditioning ourselves for victory. We both follow the formula we're about to share with you. But you know what has really empowered us to make our businesses successful until now? We make it very easy for people to deal with us. We're both instantly accessible. We talk in words of one syllable. We keep it simple because that's the way we like it. In fact, that's the only way we can cope with all the things that are simultaneously going on in our lives right now.

You know what else happens when you make it easy and simple to deal with you? You speed up the entire process. If complexity and bureaucracy are the brakes, simplicity and ease-of-use are the accelerators. Do this test for yourself. Think of all the people and companies that you hate doing business with. We bet it's because they make it difficult to deal with them. Now think of all the people and companies you enjoy dealing with. We bet you it's because you get what you want when you want it with the least amount of snot-en-trane (hassle and tears). How easy and simple do you make it for others to do business with you?

And, by the way, when someone is speaking to you and you can't understand what they're saying, you're not the one who is stupid. The other person is probably trying to make things more complicated than they need to be. They can't convince you, so they try to confuse you. The smartest people always make things very, very simple.

The ultimate mark of Spectacular Customer Service Champions is how they perform when something completely out-of-the-ordinary happens. Attitude is always the biggest obstacle.

Just before we get you excited by leading you through our Formula for Spectacular Customer Service, know that the ultimate mark of Spectacular Customer Service Champions is how they perform when something completely out-of-the-usual happens. In most companies, unusual requests are met with a blank stare, followed by a shaking of the head from side to side by the service provider. Most times, if the Customer wants to change the game, the service provider refuses to play along. So although the Customer may be forced to accept this stance, she probably isn't very happy about it. You've just lost a few points that could cost you dearly later on, especially when you had the opportunity to score heavily by playing on the same side as the Customer. Here's our basic guiding principle: if it is at all possible to give the Customer what she wants without spending vast sums of money and jeopardizing other Customers' wellbeing, then do it. Change your gameplan when the Customer changes the game. Most of the time, you'll see the requests are pretty easy to meet. The biggest obstacle is always your attitude.

The Gillis-Lipkin Formula for Spectacular Customer Service Factor One: Desire.

Without this factor, you're temporarily dead. Ultimately it's all about enthusiasm. And it all comes from knowing why you're doing what you're doing. A little Reward and Recognition will also get your motor running, but you have to know how you're doing.

Desire is the foundation for Spectacular Customer Service. Without the desire to make great service happen, nothing else will happen. The desire to serve is not something that can be forced on the service provider from the outside. It's an inside-out process. Either the fire is burning bright within you or it's not. If there's no fire, there's no warmth. And if there's no warmth, your Customers are going to go cold on you. What's more, here's a powerful truth: if there's no fire inside you, you cannot be happy. If you look into someone's eyes, you can see the fire blazing within or you can't. If you can't, it may mean that person is temporarily dead. They need something to reignite their spark before it goes out permanently. For many people, it's already too late. They are dead. They just haven't been buried yet. We're serious here. You become your habits. If you've allowed yourself to slip into a state of apathy, cynicism and pessimism, Vuka! Treat this point as a wake-up call. Don't wait another heartbeat. You don't know how much time you have left.

If all you do is demonstrate your desire, hunger and will to give a Customer spectacular service, you will probably have the edge over your competition. That's what the two of us look for when we hire staff or search for business partners: the deep inner drive to give everything they have every time they step into the service arena.

Service is not a grudge activity, *it's a way of thinking and a way of living*. Spectacular Customer Service is in a look, a touch, a word, a smile, a thought. In South Africa, though, we have a long way to go before people embrace service with this passion. For too many of us, service still equals servitude. Look at the faces of the people who serve you. Are they hot to make you happy? Are they fully committed to taking care of your every need? We think not, except in the rarest cases.

Eric Molobi, Chairman of the Kagiso Group of companies, gave us his perspective of one of the biggest service challenges in South Africa:

> *"In the Black community, our perceptions of status have been moulded by different things. For example, 50% of people in the townships would regard those who serve others in a hotel as low status people. They even have a term for people who serve in hotels or restaurants – Mathadikitchen: one who works from the kitchen. Serving others is a job that never used to carry any respect. But now it's changing. Many young people are now preparing themselves with pride for a career in hospitality and catering. So it's a sign that things are changing."*

So how do you help create the Desire, Hunger and Will in the people around you? Well, we're assuming that if you've made it this far, you're the kind of person who leads others. You may already be in a position of authority or you may be on your way there. This next message is for you.

It's not good enough being a leader, you have to be a cheerleader. Become famous for your enthusiasm. If you show that you cannot handle the stress, or if you demonstrate your anxiety, your colleagues' and Customers' morale will crumble like puff pastry.

Know this truth: you are a source of energy for everyone around you. Depending on your behaviour, you either become a positive source of energy or a negative one. We promise you that if you come to work in a bad mood, you will infect everyone around you. On the other hand, when you're happy, your joy rubs off on others. We become the company we keep. Spend time with "Down People" and you'll hit the floor. Spend time with "Up People" and you'll truly soar. What kind of person are you?

If you want to become a Spectacular Customer Service Champion, it's not good enough just being a leader – you have to be a cheerleader. You cannot afford to walk around like a bear with a sore paw. You cannot afford to indulge in your own self-pity parties. You cannot afford to give in to your disappointments or frustrations. You know why? Because other people are dependent on your mood. If you start sliding down the slippery slope of negativity, you'll pull them down with you.

If you show that you cannot handle the stress, or if you demonstrate your anxiety, your colleagues' and Customers' morale will crumble like puff pastry – especially if you are in a supervisory or managerial role. When you are in front of the people who depend on you for a living, you have to demonstrate how confident you are in the future. You have to transmit your faith and optimism at every opportunity – even when you aren't sure yourself. Customer Service champions constantly walk the motivational talk. They have the ability to rise above their negativity for the wellbeing of others. Do you?

Here's the bottom line: when you're being paid to serve somebody, your personal problems are irrelevant to her or him. You are being paid to handle their problems, not give them problems. This is harsh but true.

Here are Seven unquestionable truths of great Cheer leaders:

If you don't praise yourself, you'll end up praising no-one.
If you don't forgive yourself, you'll end up forgiving no-one.
If you don't love what you see in the mirror, you'll end up loving no-one.
If you don't say nice things to yourself, you'll end up saying nothing nice to anyone.
If you don't smile, neither will your Customers and you'll end up losing them.
If you don't act with enthusiasm, you'll end up taking it away from everyone.
If you don't treat others with joy and gratitude, you'll end up alone, miserable and broke.

The marketplace is not a charity organization: you have to be strong for others.

The marketplace is not the SPCA, it's not the YMCA and it's not the Red Cross. The marketplace doesn't care about your personal problems. It doesn't care about your marital hassles, your overdraft or your wayward teenage kids. Your Customers and colleagues don't care about your problems, they expect *you* to solve *their* problems.

So here's an important rule in the game called Success: *Don't burden others with your troubles. Don't moan about how tough things are. Don't give your Customers excuses why you didn't meet your promises.* They don't care and, what's more, your excuses will only make them angry.

We meet so many mediocre operators who are continually complaining about how tough their life is. The moment we hear the complaints start, we know this person will never make it until he changes his attitude towards life, service and his Customers. Mentally, we shut down and we look for somebody who is rising to the challenge with guts and enthusiasm.

If you are going to succeed, you need to play a number of roles. No matter what your job is, you are a social worker, a psychologist, a marriage counsellor, a big brother or sister, a best friend or soulmate, a father confessor, a shoulder to cry on or just someone to lean on when your associates are not strong.

Win your own Academy Award. If you act the part, you'll get the role.

From this moment on, treat those "Bad Mood Days" as an opportunity to strengthen your emotional muscles. If you're in a negative or subdued mood, consciously be aware of acting as though you're in a good mood. Win your own Academy Award. If you act the part, you'll get the role. Emotion is created by motion. Don't just take our word for it. Try it now: stand up. Pretend your biggest Customer is standing in front of you right now (come on, use your imagination). Take a deep breath. Put on your biggest smile. Say in a bright, cheerful voice: "I'm extremely happy to serve you." Stay smiling. How do you feel now? We know you feel better!

You know what else we've discovered? Many of us are hanging on by our fingertips. We are all stretched to the limit. We have yet to find someone who is truly cruising through life. And it's just getting tougher. That's why you have to make a superhuman effort to motivate people constantly. People have three basic needs: Security, Recognition and Love. And, whether you like it or not, you have to give them all three – even if you're not getting enough yourself. The more you give to others, the more you'll experience security, love and recognition yourself. These three magical factors cannot be bought, they cannot be ordered on demand. They have to be earned over time through constant investment of energy and effort.

Above all else, your colleagues and Customers want you to take away their psychological insecurity. No matter how old we become, there's a part of us that will always be five years old. Neglect the emotions of the people around you, and you will perish.

Good Customers and Good Colleagues are high maintenance people. They require a lot of TLC – tender loving care. They need you to pick them up, pat them on the back and hug them every now and then. This function is as important a contributor to your success in Customer Service as anything else you do. And remember, everyone is your Customer. Your boss, your colleague, your friends, your spouse and, of course, the people who buy your actual products or service.

We know what you're thinking. Some of you may not be natural expressives or extroverts. It doesn't matter. You have to do whatever you have to do in your own personal style. You have to find a way that's comfortable for you, but you have to find a way. It doesn't matter if you're quiet or if you're loud. Some of the most powerful communicators we know are softly spoken. Find your own voice and use it.

We make you this promise: *Neglect the emotions of the people around you, and you will perish.* Above all else, Customers want you to take away their psychological insecurity. They want to know that if they trust you and put their faith in you, everything will turn out well. Just think about the suppliers whom you are loyal to. What have they done to earn your loyalty? We bet they make you feel safe in an increasingly dangerous world. You feel as if you can always rely on them to come through. You know that they will never embarrass you or disappoint you. They are like Tastic Rice – they cook perfectly for you every time.

No matter how old we become, there's a part of us that will always be five years old. That's the part of us that is afraid of rejection or humiliation. People will do anything to insure themselves against these two emotions. What's more, we are so used to broken promises and being let down by others that anyone who honours their commitments will succeed.

How are you helping people cope with the Five Deadly South African Plagues: murder, rape, theft, fire and floods?

What woke you up this morning? Well, if it wasn't the neighbour's dog, and it wasn't your amorous partner, was it your alarm clock? And when your alarm went off and the radio came on, what was the first sound you heard? The news? And what was on the news? Murder, rape, theft, fire and floods. Then you listened to the news again on your way to work and what did you hear? Yup, murder, rape, theft, fire and floods. Then you got to work. And what did you hear people talk about around the coffee machine? Yup, murder, rape, theft, fire and floods. Then you heard the same bad news on your way home that evening. Then you watched the late night news on e-TV and you saw the same bad news just one more time before you went to sleep. Then what did you dream about? ? Yup, murder, rape, theft, fire and floods.

In the Business Day, February 14 2000, American Journalist Stephen Kinzer wrote the following words under the heading, "More to SA than Crime":

> *During our wonderful trip through SA recently, my family and I were typical tourists. We marvelled at the sight of big game,*

enjoyed urban night life, absorbed the beauty of the Karoo and Kalahari and even made an inspirational visit to Soweto. We were greeted warmly everywhere.

One aspect of my trip, however, was puzzling and disturbing. While we were in the car, every hour we heard a news report. These reports were alarmingly different from any I have ever heard, because they focused almost exclusively on news of violent crime.

One typical five minute report, for example, led with a double murder and continued with news of a gang rape, a kidnapping, another rape, two robberies and a shooting incident. There were two items of foreign news: a celebrity stabbing in Britain and a fatal fire in India. Every single item was about death, violence or brutality.

When people hear nothing but reports of violent crime hour after hour and day after day, they naturally develop a tremendous sense of fear and insecurity. This can lead to a national psychosis that diverts attention and energy away from the many challenges facing the country.

Every day across SA, people are doing admirable and important work that helps to galvanize society and build solidarity. Their stories are part of SA's story. By reporting these stories, the media would give readers and viewers and listeners a more accurate sense of what is happening around them. This kind of reporting might also have the effect of encouraging more people to confront and perhaps do something about their problems.

What must it do to South Africans' self image to be subjected to this relentless barrage of reports about gruesome crimes? It can only raise levels of fear beyond what is necessary and make many people wonder whether the good things in their lives are aberrations in the midst of a country enveloped in blood and violence.

So from today, be vigilant about what you choose to watch or listen to. Bad news is seductive. Bad news can also lead to feelings of futility and despair. Don't allow yourself to get sucked into the "Bad News Syndrome". Instead, you be a one-person good news station. You be the one who helps encourage and energize others. As Mahatma Gandhi said, "You be the change you seek in the world."

Seriously, we and you may not be able to change the whole country but we can change our immediate environments. As two tough minded optimists, we can promise you one thing for absolute certain: South Africans, who can help other South Africans deal with the five deadly South African plagues, will be massively successful, they will be in great demand and people will be prepared to pay them a lot of money. We talk from experience.

Do you lead by example? Are you one of the few who do versus the many who talk? When our actions are not consistent with our beliefs, we become frustrated, angry and depressed.

Time and time again, wc go into companics that promote outstanding Customer Service through posters and mission statements. However, when it comes to delivering the goods, they fall horribly short. Clearly, Spectacular Customer Service is not a priority with them. They say the words because that's what they're expected to say. And that's where it ends.

The best of the best, whether it's companies or individuals, are creatures of action. They lead by example. Almost nothing is too much trouble. They are clearly exhilarated by the opportunity to serve Customers. Even under the most trying circumstances, they sustain their composure and civility. They are the kind of people you would like to take home with you. They are role models for others. They are the few who do versus the many who talk. Are you part of this elite club? Make the decision today to join it. And you know what the best news of all is? There are no entrance fees. You decide when you've made it. All it takes is an unyielding desire to serve Customers well, coupled with the discipline to do what you know you have to do when you have to do it.

Here's a little warning you may want to heed: when our actions are not consistent with our beliefs, we become frustrated, angry and depressed. Observe the people around you. How many of them do you think are truly faithful to their beliefs? How many of them say what they mean and mean what they say? How many of them translate their words into action?

We promise you that it's the rare few. And it's usually those who are highly successful. They've discovered that there's nothing to be frightened of except themselves. The person who honours his principles dies a single death. The coward dies a thousand deaths every day.

Become famous for your enthusiasm. One of the rarest sights in South Africa today is a genuinely happy person who genuinely loves serving her Customers. If you find someone like this, compliment her. And, whatever happens, don't commit suicide by installment.

"Every memorable act in the history of the world is a triumph of enthusiasm. Nothing great was ever achieved without it because it gives any challenge or any occupation, no matter how frightening or difficult, a new meaning. Without enthusiasm you are doomed to a life of mediocrity, but with it, you can accomplish miracles."

Og Mandino

Be the kind of person who others want to be with because your spirit is so buoyant. In South Africa right now, people are being overwhelmed with problems and stress. They will flock to anyone who can light them up with hope and joy in times of darkness. And you know what? It doesn't matter whether you are selling coffee or construction, Customers are attracted to the light. So shine yours brightly.

By the way, did you know that the word "enthusiasm" comes from the Greek word, Entheos, which means Godlike. When we act with enthusiasm, we express the best part of ourselves. We are in our most alive, alert, turned on state. And that's what Customers find irresistible. In fact, they will forgive you for a lot of other shortcomings, if you act with massive enthusiasm. Even just saying the word – "en-thoo'ze-az'em" is enough to put a smile on your face.

Here's the ultimate mark of the great Customer Service Champions: they don't just have enthusiasm for 30 minutes, or 30 days or even 30 months. They have it for 30 years and more. Think about this:

"Catch on fire with enthusiasm and people will come for miles to watch you burn." *John Wesley*

So are you on fire with enthusiasm or is Customer Service just part of a job to you? Is it just something you have to do to support yourself and your family until something better comes along? Listen, we promise you that if you are just going through the motions, you are condemned to failure and unhappiness. If you are not acting with "Gees" (spirit and enthusiasm), you are busy committing suicide by installment.

How Gillis and Lipkin keep going: The K-I-F Principle – Keep It Fresh.

Every day, like millions of other South Africans, we get up and go to work. And, every day like millions of other South Africans, we have to do many of the same things we did the day before. We have to follow the discipline of our routines. Whether it's helping run a group of hotels or getting another bunch of South Africans motivated, the reality is that most of the time we have to keep doing the basics right. Just like you, we cannot afford an off-day – especially when Customers are depending on us for their success or comfort.

We admit it: there are times when both of us feel like quitting. There are times when we are truly running on empty. But then we apply the K-I-F Principle: Keep It Fresh. This principle is so simple but it's so powerful. It means:

> *When you get up in the morning, see the day ahead as the first time you're ever going to do this job. Feel the excitement and enthusiasm you first felt. Experience the exhilaration of a new start. See your challenges with fresh eyes. The day ahead is all that matters. Whatever has gone before, is gone for good – it's history. Your future depends on how you handle the next twelve hours. Let go of any bad will you have towards anyone or anything. Today, your career really takes off. Today is the day you'll perform magnificently. Today is the day you'll meet your biggest Customer ever. Today is the day you'll close your biggest deal ever. Today, anything is possible.*

Both of us are in our early forties. We have almost fifty years of Customer Service experience between us. But both of us are as excited about what we are doing today as we were the day we started. And you know what else? The Golden Thread running through all the outstanding achievers with whom we have had the privilege of working is a constant, never ending, burning romance with their jobs. Consciously or unconsciously, they keep themselves fresh by seeing their challenges and their Customers' challenges through fresh eyes.

So tomorrow morning when you wake up, decide to see your job with fresh eyes. See your Customers with fresh eyes. See your Customers' challenges with a fresh perspective. You'll be amazed at all the new solutions you'll discover. Most importantly, if you keep yourself fresh, you'll be happy. It's the difference between a freshly picked, perfect pink rose and one that was picked five days ago. Or a sizzling pizza just out the oven, or the same pizza the following morning. Or firm, bright red tomato and the same tomato a week later. If you keep yourself fresh, you'll glow and grow. If you allow yourself to go stale, you'll die. That's what we believe. What do you think? Let us know by visiting www.mikelipkin.com or fax us on (011) 728-6907.

Every company in South Africa needs an EEO like Ruth Davies.

Every company has a CEO or a COO or a CFO, but every company also needs an EEO – an Events and Encouragement Officer. An EEO is the person who is continually lifting people up when they're down. She is the one who somehow always manages to inject others with motivation and "moxie" because she has the superhuman ability to always be "Up". Almost every company has this kind of person, but not every company truly leverages the power of this kind of person. Instead, their skills and spirit are under-utilised which is a loss to everyone else in the company. Well, here's our message to you:

> *Never underestimate the power of one turned-on human being to energize the entire team. And never underestimate the power of one turned-off human being to drain the energy of the entire team. There are plenty of the latter, so celebrate and promote the former. One EEO can immunize the rest of the company against the "bad guys."*

Protea Hotel's EEO is a woman called Ruth Davies who helps run the Central Reservations Office (CRO) at the head office in Cape Town. The CRO is the nerve centre of the entire operation. The ten people who man the CRO work in a pressurized, relentless, high stress environment. The phones never stop ringing. Much of the time, they are sorting out problems. They have to be unfailingly cheerful and accurate. Any which way you look at it, their jobs are really, really tough. They always have to be cheerful and courteous to Customers.

Enter Ruth Davies. Ruth is the ultimate EEO. She was born to laugh, with a face designed to smile. When you're with her, you feel as though she's about to break into song at any moment. And, we kid you not, she does. She's always talking and singing to her people. She gets them through the rough spots by getting them to believe in themselves. She invests them with a sense of pride, togetherness and quality.

She introduces her people to themselves through the right questions. She is continually getting them to rate themselves and she does this in innovative ways. For example, when she's coaching one of her people, she'll call the person into her office. Then she'll invite her to sit behind her desk. Ruth will sit in the visitor's chair. Then she will say to the person, "If you were me and I was you, what would you advise me to do?" It gives both of them a change of perspective. The team member is encouraged to really think about herself and how she can improve. At the same time, she feels what it's like to be in Ruth's position. Both people leave the office with a greater sense of mutual understanding and learning. Hey, try it in your company. It's amazing what a different view can do.

Ruth will also organize a masseur to give her team massages during especially busy periods. Or she'll have chocolates delivered to celebrate a big or small achievement. Or she'll give each person a rose with a specially personalized message. Or she'll surprise them with a little mini-conference over breakfast at a venue nearby.

Ruth's people know that the day won't pass without something fun and enjoyable happening. She makes them want to come to work in the morning. Turnover in her team is almost zero. Their productivity is the highest in the company. They are ordinary people who have been invested with extraordinary confidence. Next to their families, Ruth is probably the most important person in her team members' lives. She has achieved the ultimate management challenge: earning both the affection and respect of her people. She has even composed the "Protea Hotels Central Reservations Theme Song" and here it is:

Sung to the tune of Perry Como's MAGIC MOMENTS

Magic Moments
Memories we're all sharing

When GUESTS phone us
They want us to be caring

Sometimes when they speak
We just want to freak
And pull out the phone lines

But all of us know
CRO is the show
Where we must shine and glow
With. . ..

MAGIC MOMENTS
Filled . . .with. . .love

Find the Ruth in your company and use her to the max. Without her, your company is Ruth-less.

Sometimes, you have to be a clown. Life is too serious to be taken seriously. Laughter is the ultimate pick-me-up. The moment your Customer smiles, you've made a breakthrough.

"I don't want to become too serious. I'm considered the clown of the

team, because I cannot be serious for two minutes. I'm afraid if I become more serious, I will stop winning." Alberto Tomba – Two Time Olympic Gold Medallist

"How do you get a Client to open up? Our number one weapon has been humour. There are now a lot of players in this market but we still break sales records every month. First we listen. Then we make our Clients feel good. We read our audience. We make it lighthearted. I've never met someone who doesn't like laughing. I listen to my Clients talk, I understand them, then I make them laugh. Humour is the vehicle but the intent must be serious. It's a balance. This is a funny and eccentric place. We try to hire people who walk that talk." Ronnie Apteker, co-founder, Internet Solutions

Sometimes, it pays to be a joker. It pays to do things that make your colleagues and your Customers laugh. Remember the power of the Court Jester: in the Middle Ages, the jester was the second most powerful person in the kingdom after the king because he made people laugh while he was telling the truth. If you truly want to capture the attention and affection of others, make sure you amuse and entertain them. But do it in a way that is respectful and appropriate.

Have you noticed how often people tend to become tense or angry over small matters? You see, it's not the thing itself that is making them tense, it's really the state they are in at that moment. We also know how easy it is to get into a rut. We've all been sucked into periods of gloom. No matter how Juiced you are, you are also human. And so are your Customers. So make them smile. Cultivate your sense of humour. Don't be afraid to make fun of yourself. Always show sensitivity to others' emotions, but at the same time, make it your mission to make your Customers smile. Over the years, both of us have worked hard to develop our sense of humour. In the hospitality and motivation industries, it's all about entertaining people. And no-one has ever been entertained without first being interested and amused.

This point is especially appropriate to those people who have a great sense of humour. If you have this skill, use it to the maximum. If you haven't, build it. But don't force it.

How a thick skin, a Pitbull determination and a sense of humour won John Henning the biggest Customer of his life.

John Henning sells catering equipment to restaurants, canteens and hotels. He is remarkably successful. But there was one Customer whom he just couldn't convert. This Customer was the buyer for one of the biggest food franchises in America. Every week, John would call this Customer and every week the Customer would tell John he wasn't interested. John tried every phone technique he knew to get an interview with him – to no avail. In fact, one morning the Customer became so irritated with John that he screamed at him to "BUGGER OFF AND STOP BUGGING ME!!!!!"

Cool as a cucumber, John called the Customer the following week and said to him, "I can't remember whether you told me to bugger off or call you to set up a meeting. I'm sure it was to set up a meeting. Am I right?" There was a pause for a moment, followed by loud laughter. The Customer agreed to see John. Today he is John's biggest account. What's the lesson John has taught us here? Never take rejection personally, never stop trying and always have a sense of humour. As John proved, the moment your Customer smiles or laughs, you've made a breakthrough. You're on the verge of making the sale and establishing an outstanding relationship.

And by the way, have you noticed how we always seem to be able to laugh at misfortune after the event. We look back at the incident and smile. Our question to you is: why wait? Laugh about it now!

Just having a little fun at Protea.

Let's face it, no matter how good a hotel is, it's not home. Most hotels can be pretty impersonal, especially if you've been away from home for a long time. What's more, one hotel is very much like the next, the only difference being a star or two under the hotel name. Protea recognized this and set out to differentiate themselves by introducing little dabs of humour on items commonly found in hotel rooms. Their thinking was that if they can make the Guest smile, they make the Guest's experience more enjoyable. And if the Guest's experience is more enjoyable, the Guest is more likely to come back. We can't argue with that logic. For your enjoyment, here are some of the little dabs of humour you're likely to find at a Protea Hotel:

On Glass Coasters
What colour does a Smurf turn when you choke him?
If a synchronized swimmer drowns, do the rest have to drown too?
Would a fly without wings be called a walk?
The severity of the itch is proportional to the reach!
If cops arrest a mime, do they tell him he has the right to remain silent?
He who laughs last thinks slowest.
If love is blind, why is lingerie so popular?
No one is listening until you make a mistake.

Toilet roll stickers
Tear on dotted line.
97 sheets to go.
Panado
She has no excuse now.

Soap
Wash behind your ears, love Mom.
Shampoo
Left handed shampoo.
Foam bath
Just add partner and mix.
Body lotion
Think of it as shampoo for bald people.
Cleaner's trolley
How's my driving? Dial nine for reception.
Fire escape sign
We don't have a gym. Please feel free to run up and down the stairs.

If we can see you smile and hear you chuckle, we're already halfway to making you come back.

Humour keeps you humble. The person you really need to laugh at is yourself.

We guarantee you that the number one reason why you become angry, indignant or outraged, is that you take yourself too seriously. Just like you, we are guilty of this tendency at times. And every time we think that we're more important than we really are, or every time we think that we're error-proof, along comes a massive AAK to set us right – that's an Attitude Adjustment Klap from above.

Watch people who lose their temper easily or who get upset easily, we bet it's because they haven't learnt to laugh at themselves. We promise you this: if you cannot laugh at yourself in South Africa right now, you're a heart attack waiting to happen. There's too much intensity on the outside for us not to relax on the inside. That's why Angels can fly – it's because they take themselves lightly. On the other hand, if you take yourself too seriously, you'll be very heavy even if you are my brother.

Peter Sheahan.

One of Mike's role models is a man called Peter Sheahan who is a Financial Consultant with Royal Bank in Ottawa, Canada. He is highly successful, managing a portfolio of over $35 million of Customers' funds. Peter moves around in a wheelchair after having severely injured himself in a sporting accident. When Peter phones a Prospect, he usually gets an appointment because of his professionalism and charming phone manner. However, when he meets the Customer for the first time, he can usually see the shock and discomfort etched all over the Customer's face. Peter immediately applies his sense of humour to put the Customer at ease. He knows that if he can get the Customer to smile, the Customer will begin to relax and Peter will be able to apply his knowledge and experience to the Customer's benefit. "Until that first smile,"says Peter, "there is discomfort and tension. After that smile, the Customer looks at me as someone just like him who has gone through a major life challenge." There but for the Grace of God go all of us.

So learn to joke with yourself. Unless you're a doctor who is in the business of saving lives, whatever you're doing can't be all that serious. And unless you've just been involved in a near fatal accident, whatever has just happened can't be that serious either. Here's a true story that puts this all in perspective. It is one of the most inspiring stories we have ever read. When a person's life is at stake, you never, ever, ever give up:

Young doctor fights to revive clinically dead patient.

Johannesburg, Thursday 24 December 1999. It was the day before Christmas when an elated Susanna van Rooyen left the old age home in Boksburg to be with her family. At the time she could not possibly imagine that in less than an hour she would be brought back from the brink of death by a group of strangers.

The 72 year-old Susanna felt fantastic that morning. The only thing on her mind was being ready for her son, Pieter, who was fetching her for the Christmas weekend. She got into the car with him and started chattering away like the happy grandmother that she was. All of a sudden, she went silent. Pieter looked at her and immediately saw that something was desperately wrong. In a state of shock, the only thing he could think of was to get his mother to the Medicross Clinic as fast as possible. With his hand on the hooter and his hazard lights flashing, Pieter put his foot flat on the accelerator and drove the three kilometres to the hospital. But it was the busiest time of the year and, as he fought his way through the dense traffic, he saw that his mother had slid all the way down in her seat and stopped breathing.

A few minutes later he arrived at the clinic. He leapt from his car and sprinted into the clinic shouting, "My mother, my mother, please help my mother!" Two quick-thinking receptionists sprang into action without hesitation. The first followed him to his car with a wheelchair while the other alerted the staff in the procedures room. When Susanna arrived in the Medicross procedures room, 25 year old Dr Zayd Mohamed took control. It looked tragic. Susanna had no heartbeat. She had been clinically dead for some minutes.

Undeterred, the young doctor and his team of five nursing sisters set out to produce a miracle and bring her back to life. Several minutes later, after using every tool at their disposal, including a little prayer, they detected a faint heartbeat. The battle had been won. Six people working together as one, united by a common purpose – saving a woman's life, had indeed done the impossible.

Dr Mohamed didn't even believe he deserved any praise. "The staff of the clinic, and in particular, the Medicross nursing sisters deserve all the kudos," he said. "It was nothing like those scenes you see in the movies. Hardly a word was spoken. We just went about our work with each and every person quietly and efficiently doing what needed to be done."

The story has a happy ending. Susanna recovered from her ordeal and, at the time of writing, she is doing well.

We hope that this story has put your daily activities in a different light. How would you have handled the challenge that faced Dr Mohamed and his team? So we say to you once again, if a human life is not at stake, chill. Relax. Smile. Laugh. Chuckle. And help your colleagues and Customers do the same.

In fact, if we said to you right now that we could give you a foolproof way of taking away your Customer's anger and annoyance almost every time, would you be interested? Of course you would. So here it is: make a joke of yourself in the heat of the moment, the Customer will melt in front of you and you'll be Juiced!

Tell people why they're doing what they're doing and they'll find their desire by themselves. Purpose is Power. And if they're not working on purpose, they're working by accident.

Quick, tell us in one sentence why we should do business with you. What is the number one benefit we're going to get from your company that we wouldn't get from anyone else? Why do you get up in the morning to go to work? What's the driving force that keeps you moving forward when you are faced with one problem after another? What are the values that drive you and your company? What's your and your company's code of conduct? How do you know what's important and what's not in your company?

If you struggled to answer any one of the above questions, know you're not alone. Most the people we interview on these issues cannot give us a definite response. They don't have a clear picture of what their purpose really is. So they slog through their tasks every day without the personal power that comes from having a compelling reason to do what they're doing.

We promise you this: if your people don't know why

they're really doing what they're doing, they cannot act with true passion and enthusiasm. For example, if you're a salesperson at a clothing retailer and you see yourself as someone who merely helps Customers find what they're looking for, you'll always be mediocre. However, if you know you work for a company that wants to be the number one Customer Service company in the world and your role is to make your Customers feel outstanding by looking outstanding, you'll play at a higher level and help all those around you do the same. By the way, what level are you playing at right now? If we were to observe you at work, would your energy and enjoyment levels blow us away? Or would we see yet another service provider merely complying with the rules and doing just enough to keep his job?

Let's say you sell cars for a living and you see your job as making enough commission to live well. Do you think you'll really perform with Juice? Or will you fight a constant battle with demotivation, frustration and fatigue? On the other hand, if your purpose is to make Customers' lives more exciting by getting them into the cars you're selling, because you truly believe that your car is the finest driving machine they can get for their money, do you think you'll be able to act with more Juice? Definitely!

Our purpose through our seminars and this book is to make people massively successful by giving them the tools and insights to deliver spectacular service to others. We want to get people so excited that they do those things that they were previously unable or afraid to do. The thought of thousands of South Africans going out there and stepping up to a higher level while inspiring others to do the same, fills us with a great sense of pleasure. That's why we're so Juiced! Just thinking of you reading these words gets our motors running.

What really Juices you?

No matter who you are or where you are in the company, if there is no definite, inspiring purpose, go to the leadership of the company today and start the process of creating one. Don't be shy. Don't be backward in coming forward. We promise you that if you seize this kind of initiative, you will be well rewarded – as long as you never give up. Don't stop at the first obstacle. And even if you experience delays in helping create a corporate purpose, create your own personal purpose today. It could be the most powerful action you ever take. Simply ask yourself the following four self-power questions:

What really Juices me?
What am I really good at?
How can I use my gifts to help others?
What's most important to me in my life?

Don't worry if the answer doesn't come to you straight away. Think seriously about these self-power questions and your subconscious mind will help you find the answers.

Of course, if you are a senior member or owner of a company reading these words and you haven't yet crafted a Purpose and set of Values for your company, now would be an excellent time to start. As importantly, the process by which you arrive at your purpose must include all your people. Involve them at the beginning and they'll be with you until the end.

The Anthony Robbins Companies Trainer Code of Conduct.

Anthony Robbins is one of America's leading motivators and personal performance coaches. He runs a group of companies which are all market leaders in their fields. Mike attended a training programme of his in San Diego, California at the end of 1999. While he was there he was exposed to the Code of Conduct to which the trainers of Anthony Robbins have to adhere. We thought this Code was so outstanding we've shared it with you here:

In keeping with my commitment to maintain the Anthony Robbins standard of excellence, I will adhere to a specific set of ethics and behaviour.

I resolve to:

- *Dress in a professional manner. Clothes will be clean and appropriate for the occasion or event.*
- *Be punctual for all events and meetings. I will return phone calls in a timely manner.*
- *Be completely accountable for my actions and responsible for my consequences, recognizing that I am the only one who is in control of both.*
- *Support Tony Robbins in making the event a Class 1 experience for all participants.*
- *Treat everyone with respect and compassion.*
- *Be of service to all involved. I understand that we are here for the participants and for their greater good, and realize the greatest gift I have is that of giving. Leadership is all about expanding and contributing.*
- *Exercise and be an outstanding example of wellness, sensory acuity and common sense. I will be open to feedback and praise because I know that is how I grow and contribute.*
- *Recognize that I am a role model and an example of the technology that we teach, therefore my physical condition does make a difference; not only on how I impact others, but with my own energy level and quality of life as well.*

Do you have a similar code of conduct that governs behaviour and attitude towards Customers in your company? Do you have a personal code of conduct for yourself?

The Greatest Management Principle in the World: Reward the behaviour that you want more of and you'll see a lot more of it.

Many of the companies that we go into suffer from an acute case of schizophrenia. Management says one thing, then rewards another. They're in two minds about Spectacular Customer Service. They preach the gospel of Customer Relationship Management – CRM, the new buzz term of the 2000's. They evangelize the need to build long term, intimate emotional connections with Customers. Salespeople are told to be consultative and interdependent, but they're rewarded purely on the basis of units sold or expenses saved, irrespective of their impact on Customer relationships. Their reward system is in direct contradiction to what they're being asked to do.

What's more, winner-take-all incentives are often introduced for salespeople. The best salesperson wins a trip to an exotic location. Or the best performer wins the trophy at the annual conference and walks away with a big fat cheque for her efforts.

Many companies don't even know what their Customers think of them. What's more, they're too scared to ask because they're afraid of the response they'll get. So the Customer Service Champions go the extra mile after mile after mile with no reward or recognition from management.

Here's the key insight: there is often a lag between the service initiative and the result. Secondly, it's initiative on top of initiative on top of initiative that builds a great Customer relationship over time. If people were incentivised to keep generating those initiatives, you would see a lot more people become a lot more creative.

So are your business processes oriented towards rewarding employees who give their all to their Customers? Is there a system in place that catches these champions doing things right in their pursuit of Spectacular Customer Service? Examine your business. If your answer to these questions is "no", take action this second to change them. We promise you there is nothing else you can do in your business that will give you a higher return on investment.

You cannot spend enough money rewarding your service stars. FNB paid Jacqueline le Roux R1-million.

If you are serious about improving Customer Service, reward those people who deliver spectacular Customer Service. And reward them lavishly. You cannot spend enough money rewarding your service stars. They're the lifeblood of your business and yet, most of the time, they're taken for granted, especially if they're not in sales where they'll eventually be rewarded simply by selling more.

So if we were standing in front of you right now and we asked you how you reward your service stars, what would your response be? Do you even have a reward structure in place? Do you even have a feedback system in place? Are you constantly going out of your way to celebrate and congratulate your stars? How much money are you investing in them? How often do you reward them? How many parties have you had in the past three months to recognize them? How creative are you in finding ways to celebrate your service stars? FNB got very creative with Jacqueline le Roux:

> *A 22 year old bank clerk from sleepy Fort Beaufort in the Eastern Cape saved her employer, FNB, a little more than R3000 recently – and has been rewarded for her honesty with a cool million.*
>
> *Employed at FNB for only four months, Jacqueline le Roux*

became an instant millionaire in an FNB lucky draw for employees who blow the whistle on fraud. Employees who report fraud are entered in the monthly draw and the winner takes home between R25 000 and R1-million in prize money.

Le Roux, chosen from 1064 entries, spotted a Customer's cheque that had been fraudulently inflated from R460 to R4 600. She was flown up to Johannesburg (her very first time in an airplane) and accommodated at the luxurious Hilton Hotel. Needless to say, she was thrilled. Le Roux also said she had no plans to leave the employer who has made her so wealthy.

Now, obviously not every company has the resources of FNB. But what we loved about this story was the commitment and creativity behind the reward. FNB are serious about cutting down on fraud and they demonstrate their seriousness in recognizing people who come forward. Are you? Gordon Joffe, Managing Director of Polo Clothing, Cape Town, South Africa is. And it cost him a lot less than a million rand.

Joffe's challenge was to sensitize his people to the merits of good service and the consequences of poor service. He shared his principles of good internal service with his supervisors. Then, at the end of the year Christmas party, he surprised his people by announcing three awards for the supervisors who delivered the best service to their people. The first prize was R2 000, the second prize was R1 000 and the third was R500.

It was the first time an initiative of this nature was implemented in the company and the supervisors loved it. The reaction amazed Joffe. The winners collected their awards to thunderous applause. Although only three supervisors won the award, it was as if all the supervisors were being recognized. This simple event has made a massive difference to the motivation of the supervisors at Polo Clothing. What simple initiatives can you introduce to make a massive difference in your company?

There is always going to be a "Reward-Deficit". Catch yourself doing things right and find the applause within. The rewards will follow. Delays are not denials. The real rewards are always the rewards you give to yourself: work is play and play is work.

There is no organization in the world that gives its people all the praise and recognition they feel they deserve. In fact, let's ask you this question: how many people do you know who are overpaid and underworked? Almost all the people we speak to believe that they deserve more rewards – more money, more praise, more recognition, more support.

Know this truth: there is always going to be a "Reward-Deficit". If you aspire to being an authentic super-performer, recognize the fact now that no-one is going to thank you enough. If you're relying on others to keep you motivated, you're always going to feel miserable. It's up to you to catch yourself doing things right and find the applause within to keep going when the going gets tough. At the same time, it's up to you to keep giving as much as you can to the people around you – even when no-one is giving to you. The mere act of giving will energize you. James Michener expressed it best when he wrote:

> *"The master in the art of living makes little distinction between his work and his play, his labour and his leisure, his mind and his body, his information and his recreation, his love and his religion. He hardly knows which is which. He simply pursues his vision of excellence at whatever he does, leaving others to decide whether he is working or playing. To him, he's always doing both."*

But here's the good news: we promise that if you've got what it takes and you do what it takes over the long term, you will be rewarded. And you will be rewarded hugely. It takes stamina and it takes tenacity. It also takes a little bit of luck. And the more you deliver, the luckier you get.

If you truly want to get your people to perform, get their peers to show them how. If one South African can, another South African can.

Rewards, as we all know, are not just about money. They're about recognition. Here's a big idea that is so simple and so inexpensive: consistently profile your winners and your Customer Service champions. Interview them. Videotape them. Play the videos to the rest of the business. Interview and videotape Customers who have been served and delighted by these people. Run small ads in the local newspapers celebrating these people. Make them heroes. Make them celebrities within your company. Make them role models for others to follow.

If you truly want your people to perform, show them how well their peers are doing. Don't show a South African how well an American or Argentinean is performing a certain task. It will have limited relevance at best. Instead, find your best performer and make her the model for others. If one South African can, another South African can.

The Leadership needs to eat their own dogfood. If a picture is worth a thousand words, then an act is worth a million. The centre of gravity needs to be lowered to the frontline. Beware of the curse of success.

Both of us have read book after book on how we should all get our staff to become obsessive about caring for the Customer. (Please note that we haven't used this word once. Obsession in any form is not a pretty sight). Here's what we believe: you can be a one-person business or you can be Anglo-American, but the primary responsibility of serving Customers always rests on the shoulders of the leadership of the company.

The actions, words and behaviour of the people at the top will determine whether the rest of the company takes Customer Service seriously. That's why memos and e-mails telling people to serve Customers better will have little effect. What will have a major effect is the sight of top management on the ground-floor serving Customers. Nothing will impress people more than seeing management walking their talk at the rockface. Management needs to eat their own dogfood or they will not be taken seriously. We see it all the time. If a picture is worth a thousand words, then an act is worth a million. Lead from the front and the troops will follow. And yet the sight of leaders at grassroots level is still extremely rare. Carol Scott, Executive Chairlady of Imperial Car Rental, expressed it well when she said in an interview with Style Magazine (May 2000): "Don't expect your staff to do something that you won't. Don't sit in an Ivory Tower. Answer your own phone. Work alongside your people."

We see it all the time: companies become successful because they're in love with their Customers. They love to serve and they show it. Then as their businesses grow, the key people have less and less time to spend with their Customers. Their passion isn't passed on and the rot sets in just as the company is at its most successful. Is this happening to you or your company? Of course not. You would never allow it. Are we right?

By the way, if you are a frontline service person and you see this curse beginning to make its ugly presence in your company – talk up. If your company is worth working for, management will love and respect you for it. Remember, fortune favours the brave.

Ignorance is not bliss. It's deadly. Feedback is the breakfast of Customer Service champions. You cannot have desire without feedback.

"You can't care too much about your Customers, you can only care too little. You can't drive a Customer crazy with attention. You can

only make him crazy through lack of attention. Call the Customer every day, they love it."

Ronnie Apteker, co-founder, Internet Solutions

How much feedback are you getting from your Customers? We don't know about you, but we can't remember the last time any one of our suppliers asked us what we think of them. Seriously, both of us are big users of a wide range of services. in both our professional and personal lives. And yet, hardly anyone calls us to find out if we're happy with their services. All it takes is a weekly phone call. Even a call every fortnight would be impressive. The first supplier that takes this initiative will score big points with us. What's more, they'll actually find out what we think of them and they'll be able to take action.

For many of us, there is almost nothing worse than lack of attention. Although we may vent our emotions if we're not happy when a supplier asks for feedback, we're secretly pleased and delighted that someone even cares enough to call. So, are you calling your Customers every week or even every day?

We know that many of the companies who've bought this book have sophisticated research programmes that track Customers' opinions, likes and dislikes, consumption habits, tastes and other "important" data. The question we're asking you here is: how often are you personally talking to a Customer about your performance? How often do you look into their eyes or listen to them talk live to you about your service delivery? Are you running for cover? Or are you prepared to face the storm? And you know what? It's never as bad as you think it's going to be. We promise you one thing, though, if you don't get the feedback, the alternatives are far, far worse. One day, the Customer will just up and leave you without a second glance. That's pain.

Every month, 10 000 Guests actually take the trouble to fill out the cards. That tells you something about peoples' desire to have their voices heard.

The two of us run very different businesses. Arthur helps lead a group of over 120 hotels employing over 12 000 people. Mike runs a motivation and publishing company called Touch The Sky, employing less than ten people. But their common denominator is a huge commitment to feedback of both the formal and the informal kind.

Protea Hotels process over 10 000 Customer Comment cards a month. That means 10 000 Guests actually take the trouble to fill out the cards. That tells you something about peoples' desire to have their voices heard. They also fill out these cards because Protea makes it easy for them. The cards are in their rooms. There are five simple questions relating to: service; comfort and cleanliness; bathroom; food and beverage; and overall performance. The Guests are also promised that every card will be followed up. The cards are signed by and addressed to Otto Stehlik, Executive Chairman of the Group.

The cards are then forwarded to head office where the Guest's name is captured and every card is responded to. The results are then plotted on a graph and compared to the group average. Each individual hotel has to set monthly improvement targets in order to achieve or exceed group benchmarks. Protea also has a team that does a quality audit on each hotel one to two times per year.

Phew! Does that sound complicated or what? Well, if you're a large company, you can probably identify with that kind of process. However, if you're a tiny company like Mike's Touch The Sky, you probably can't. What Mike does is very simple: after each seminar, he calls the Customer to get feedback. He also faxes or e-mails a five-question questionnaire to them requesting feedback on content, usefulness, enjoyability, venue and overall impression. It's easy. It's quick. All Mike does is ask Customers to rate him out of ten on each criterion and give a brief comment. 80% of all Customers complete the questionnaire. It's also extremely useful. Here's why: Mike wants to maintain an approval rating of 90% or higher on every seminar. If he drops below that score, he wants to take immediate remedial action. Without that kind of information, it's easy to slip into mediocrity. Anonymity and insolvency follow very soon after.

Our key point here is that it's not the process that's important. It's identifying the key points that are crucial to your business. It's the relentless commitment to feedback. It's the willingness to take action on the results. And it's the desire to keep getting better and better.

Make it easy for your Customers to compliment you and your people. And if you want to receive Spectacular Customer Service, compliment the people who serve you. Be kind to strangers, you never know when you're talking to an Angel.

Yes, asking for feedback is vital. But, making it easy for your Customers to compliment you or your people can be as important. At the Best Western Inn of Chicago, a budget priced hotel on the North Shore of the city, Guests are provided with a card with their checkout bill which reads:

> *"Did any one employee make your stay at the Inn of Chicago memorable? Please fill out this Star Card and leave it at the front desk."*

What are you doing to direct your Customers' attention towards individual acts of Spectacular Customer Service by your employees? You see, if you don't specifically turn your Customers' focus towards the magic moments of their interaction with you, they will automatically focus on the tragic moments. That's just the way human beings are. 99% of the time, things can be handled superbly. But the Customer will remember the awful 1% of the time when a mistake was made. And most of the time, the employee involved in the "awful 1%" will be reprimanded.

So when you introduce a device to make it easy for the Customers to compliment you and your people, you achieve two objectives. Firstly, you get your Customers to focus on the highlights of your service delivery and, secondly, you massively motivate your employees by letting them know that they are appreciated by both the company and the Customer.

And remember, if you want to receive Spectacular Customer Service, compliment the people who are serving you. Walk your own talk. Seize every opportunity to reinforce excellence wherever you encounter it. Be your own motivator and coach. Seriously, you will discover that people become very emotional. They will either smile and blush with pleasure or they may even cry. Think about yourself. Remember the last time someone paid you a sincere, unexpected compliment. Didn't you get just a little emotional?

We practise this principle all the time and it pays massive dividends. Not only do we tend to receive preferential service, but other opportunities manifest themselves in the most surprising ways: recently, Mike flew back to Johannesburg from Durban on SAA. While he was waiting in the queue to check in, he studied the ground hostess who was extremely courteous, humorous and efficient in the way she interacted with the passengers she was checking onto the flight. When it was Mike's turn to check in, he gave her a sincere compliment, commenting on all the things he had observed while he was waiting in line. She looked at Mike speechless. Then her eyes moistened and a little tear trickled down her cheek. She told Mike that he was the first person who had ever paid her such a nice compliment.

Here's the best part of the story: unknown to Mike, the Managing Director of a large company was standing behind him in the queue. He saw Mike motivate the ground hostess to tears. He was so impressed that two weeks later he hired Mike to conduct a series of seminars with his people across South Africa.

You never know who is watching you. But what you always know is that no good, kind, generous, sincere act goes unnoticed or unrewarded. The opposite, however, is also true: if you are nasty to people or you lose your temper with them, you will pay dearly for your bad behaviour sometime soon.

Who are the most important Customers you need to get feedback from? The Customers who've just fired you or decided not to use you. What's more, just by asking for feedback, you can motivate them to give you business in the future.

If you're like us, we know that you're a highly competitive human being. You want to win so badly, you can taste it. That's your edge. You hunger for the victory. You'll do almost anything, whenever and wherever you need to, to get the business. Nothing, absolutely nothing, comes even close to signing the deal, winning the Customer, and thrashing the competition. Defeat is too horrible to even contemplate. The thought of your competitor in bed with your Customer is like your worst nightmare come true.

That's why it's so hard to even talk to a Customer who has decided not to go with you, or worse, has fired you. We know the feeling. Despite our best efforts, we experience it almost every day. But what we also know is that these are the Customers who we must speak to. They hold the key to our ability to deliver Spectacular Customer Service in the future.

You know why? Because they will tell you what you should have done or what you shouldn't have done to get their business. They will give you a very different point of view on your performance. They will highlight the gaps in your delivery process that you need to fill. In short, they have valuable gifts for you but you have to ask for them.

What's more, because it's so rare, if you ask for feedback in the right way, you plant the seed for future business. By asking for feedback, you have let the Customer know how important he is to you; you have demonstrated your desire to learn and grow; and you've displayed courage and professionalism. You've also demonstrated your foresight. Your challenge is not just to make the sale, it's to build a quality relationship with the Customer over time. Today's setback may be tomorrow's celebration.

Burn your fear of rejection.

Why do you think most people don't call their Prospects for feedback? We believe it's because they think they've been personally rejected by the Prospect in the first place. And what do we all fear almost as much as death itself? Yup, rejection. Well, here's what we believe: the reason why you didn't get the business probably had very little to do with you personally. The Prospect didn't give the business to someone else just to spite you. He may have felt more comfortable with your competition because they may have packaged their proposal more attractively or they may have caught him on a better day than you or they may be related to him through a fifth cousin. The reality is that there is a range of possible reasons why you didn't get the business. So make a vow never to fear rejection again. In fact, right now, we want you to literally burn your fear of rejection. Take a piece of paper and write down these four words: "My fear of rejection". Now light a match or take a lighter and burn them. If that is all this book does for you, we'll know we've made a big contribution to your future.

You know what else? Every time you do something that is really hard, you build your character and your capacity to do even more. Whatever has happened has happened. So don't just accept it, embrace it. Make it work for you. To quote Napoleon Hill, the great motivator and author of the bestselling book, Think and Grow Rich:

> *Every adversity has within it the seed of an equal or greater benefit.*

A case study: you can lose the sale intelligently or stupidly. If you lose it intelligently, you haven't really lost anything. You've just prepared yourself to win a bigger piece of business in the future. Intelligently means that you'll get an even bigger sale in the future. Stupidly means that you'll never do business with that Customer again. Here's a specific illustration of this vital principle: Protea is continually pitching for big conferences against some very good competition in a very tight marketplace. Now let's say, despite their best efforts, Protea loses a big pitch to the competition. They clearly lose the sale. What should they do? Let's say that you're the Managing Director of Protea Hotels, what would you do? Here's what Arthur does with his team:

Firstly, they call the Customer and say, "Thank you for the opportunity to pitch on your business." Here Protea keep the door open by expressing their gratitude to the Customer for even putting Protea on the initial shopping list.

Secondly, they say to the Customer, "In choosing Hotel X, we think you've made a great decision. However, our hotel is there for you if you require anything, whether it's additional rooms or a theme evening. Is there anything else that we can do?" It's very important to congratulate the Customer on making a good decision. The worst thing that Protea could have done is badmouth their competition. That would have been game-over. What's known as the "accessory" pitch then followed. Protea are positioning themselves firstly as a possible resource for the Customer and secondly as the place the Customer will use if their primary venue can't meet their needs. Importantly, by delivering the accessory pitch, Protea are taking away some of the Customer's psychological insecurity and thereby winning the Customer's goodwill.

Thirdly, a week before the conference, Protea call the Customer and wish him good luck for his conference. Once again, though, Protea will offer their service to the Customer if he needs them. Arthur's objective here is to impress the Customer with Protea's professionalism, follow up and consistency.

Finally, a week after the event, Protea will call the Customer to find out how the conference went and to offer them their services in the future. This initiative achieves three objectives – firstly, it sustains the relationship even though there was no sale; secondly, if the competition didn't perform, Protea find out about it; thirdly, there is a strong likelihood that this Customer's company may be having another conference in the near future. If so, Protea get an immediate bite at that cherry. Finally, the follow-up, despite the fact that the sale wasn't even made in the first place, will greatly impress the Customer.

One thing is for absolutely certain, this Customer will be having another conference. This Customer will want a change. This Customer will call Protea. It's called making the sale in the future. The initial pitch was therefore not "lost", it was just a foundation for a far bigger piece of the Customer's business tomorrow. Protea will stay on this Customer's radar and keep romancing them until they get the sale.

The Gillis-Lipkin Formula for Spectacular Customer Service Factor Two: Empathy.

It's all about the passion to serve. Follow St. Francis of Assisi, the Patron Saint of Customer Service. Get into Rapport – We all need to be social chameleons. Suffer fools gladly. Chunk down. Deepen your involvement.

If there is one woman who epitomized the passion to serve, it was Mother Theresa. It may seem strange featuring such a woman in a book on Customer Service. But Mother Theresa personified empathy more than any other person over the past 100 years. She dedicated most of her life to helping people die with dignity. When everyone had failed them, Mother Theresa and the Missionary Sisters of Charity were there for them in their last hours.

Arthur Gillis and Mike Lipkin are about as far away from Mother Theresa as Canada is from Cape Town. But we share one thing in common with her: we have a passion to serve, to serve in a very different way, but to serve. We particularly like the following prayer written by St Francis of Assisi which Mother Theresa and her order followed every day. Keep this prayer close to you. We believe it should be said daily by every person in Customer Service everywhere. In fact, we'd like to anoint St Francis of Assisi as the Patron Saint of Customer Service:

> ***The St Francis of Assisi Customer Service Prayer (to be said at the start of every working day)***
>
> *Lord, make me an instrument of your peace:*
> *where there is hatred, let me sow love;*
> *where there is injury, pardon;*
> *where there is doubt, faith;*
> *where there is despair, hope;*

where there is darkness, light;
where there is sadness, joy.
Lord, may I not so much seek
To be consoled as to console;
To be understood as to understand;
To be loved as to love.
Because it is in giving that we receive,
In pardoning that we are pardoned.

Empathy means stepping into the other person's shoes and caring more about them than you do about yourself. That's why women are taking over: they have a far greater capacity for empathy than men do.

Have you noticed that you will do far more for people whom you care about than you will for yourself? At the same time, have you noticed how sensitive you are to the feelings and concerns of those people whom you love, cherish and admire? On the other hand, have you noticed how insensitive you are to people you do not like? Have you noticed that you feel nothing for their discomfort? In certain cases, have you noticed that you even get a sense of perverse pleasure when you read about the discomfort of those people you don't like?

The difference between empathy and apathy is simply how much you care about the other person and the results you want to achieve for them. Where there is no care, there cannot be Spectacular Customer Service. Where people are selfish and self-centred, there cannot be Spectacular Customer Service. Where people are unhappy, there cannot be Spectacular Customer Service, because Spectacular Customer Service requires a massive dose of empathy. And when people are too tired or turned off, they go numb. They are unable to empathize with others. They're so concerned about their own wellbeing that they have no more space for anyone else. As Vince Lombardi said, "Fatigue makes cowards of us all."

On the other hand, where Spectacular Customer Service is the ultimate goal, you'll usually find it. Where there is a spirit of teamwork and Ubuntu, you'll find it too. And when people are Juiced, you'll definitely find it. In fact, we believe the level of Customer Service is directly related to the level of joy and optimism in the organization. It's far easier to be empathetic and caring if you feel cared for. It's far easier to step into someone else's shoes if you're sure your own shoes will be there when you return.

The level of empathy in a company is a key barometer of the company's health. Put this statement to the test. Compare the service of those companies with high empathy to those where people care very little about each other. We'd bet that the high empathy companies win every time.

And by the way, that's why women are rising to the top in unprecedented numbers: they have a far greater capacity for empathy than men. Empathy seems to be built into the female psyche whereas for men, it's a rare trait. When it comes to Spectacular Customer Service, more and more the right man for the job will be a woman.

Empathy also means seeing reality through the Customer's eyes: the story of a room with a different view.

Recently, Protea received a comment from a particular Guest who said that room 209 at the Protea Hotel Knysna was absolutely terrible. This Guest was extremely angry with Protea. He said that the hotel was disgusting, the staff were bad and the entire experience was shocking. As Arthur was about to respond to the Guest, another Guest comment was forwarded to him. By a strange coincidence, it was also written by a Guest who had stayed in room 209 at the

Protea Hotel Knysna, just two days after the first unhappy Guest. However, this Guest and her husband had had a wonderful stay. Arthur called both Guests to find out what happened from their point of view.

He discovered that the first Guest had driven to Knysna from Johannesburg to make a business presentation. However, when he arrived in Knysna, he found out that his meeting had been postponed. He was frustrated and exhausted when he checked into the hotel. So when he saw the Guest comment card, he really vented his emotions and let rip.

The second Guest was a German woman who was touring the Garden Route with her husband. They arrived at the hotel after visiting another Protea Hotel just 30 minutes drive away. They were having the holiday of a lifetime and they just loved room 209, the hotel and all the staff. They had a different view.

The room, the hotel and the staff were the same but the Guests' perception was different. Who was right? Both of them. They saw reality through different emotional and attitudinal lenses. The moral of this story is that all of us are really in the business of managing our Customer's moods. We need to empathize with Customers and then handle them accordingly. So how well tuned are your antennae? How effective are you at responding to Customers' moods? How flexible are you in moving from one mood to another – depending on your Customers?

Here's the Gillis-Lipkin Platinum Customer Service Rule: *Demonstrate your empathy with the Customer's mental state by expressing your understanding of how he feels and what he wants.* Nothing will endear you to a Customer more than showing him how much you understand him. So how can you do this in your business?

If I hear you correctly, what you're really saying to me is. . .

When Mike is pitching to a Customer, he has to immediately demonstrate that he understands the challenges facing his people. Often, the Customer isn't even sure what he wants. In fact, he may even be depending on Mike to help clarify his thinking. Recently, Mike was in Chicago pitching to a large professional services company. He asked the Prospect her opinion on the biggest challenge facing her company. She responded by saying "Fear of change."

Mike probed a little more and discovered that the Prospect's Customers wanted her company to provide innovative solutions to brand new e-centric problems. He put the two together and said to the Prospect with strength and sincerity, "If I hear you correctly, what you're really saying to me is that your people need to act with confidence and boldness. However, because they're scared themselves, they aren't managing their Customers with authority and leadership. My role would be to help your people discover their personal power, realize that they have all the resources they need to lead their Customers and motivate them to unleash their creativity with conviction. Am I right?"

The Prospect just looked at Mike, smiled and said, "If you can do that, you've got the job!" Of course, Mike never overpromises. He won the assignment and made good on his commitment. But what really persuaded the Prospect to go with Mike was Mike's ability to express his understanding of what she really wanted. Mike knew that he was dealing with someone who was scared herself. Her job was on the line. His role was to reassure the Prospect and help her help her colleagues. How can you do the same with your Customers?

The Magic of Rapport – the Master Tool of Spectacular Customer Service. Practise the Juiced! Rule of Spectacular Customer Service.

If empathy is the root, then Rapport is the nourishment of great relationships. People who have the ability to achieve Rapport with others instantly will consistently deliver Spectacular Customer Service.

So what is this magical thing called Rapport? First of all, it's not a newspaper. Rapport is when two or more people connect with each other in a harmonious, mutually trusting and rewarding way. It's when you feel as though the other person or people really, really identify with you, like you, respect you and want to help you. Rapport is when you thoroughly enjoy being with another person because you know she is very similar to you in her values, beliefs and behaviour. Have you ever felt like that with others? How long did it take you to get that comfortable with them? Sometimes it happened in a heartbeat. Are we right? Well, the Customer Service Champions have the ability to spark Rapport with every Customer instantly, and we'll show you how to do that now.

Think about this: have you ever said to yourself, "I like this person because we've got big differences"? We don't think so. On the other hand, how many times have you said, "I like that person because we've got so much in common"? Remember the fundamental law of Rapport: people like to be with people who are like they are or how they would like to be. We all need to be social chameleons and change our styles according to the people we serve.

We see so many people in Customer Service fail because they failed to build Rapport. They just didn't "talk the other person's language". They didn't respect or integrate into the other person's culture. As a result, they remained strangers. No emotional bond was established. To build Rapport, you have to adapt your personality, posture and words to those of the other person. And you have to do it instantly. It doesn't mean being hypocritical and it doesn't mean being insincere. It also doesn't mean trying to be what you are not. It does mean being versatile and flexible. So practise the Juiced! rule of Spectacular Customer Service:

> *Do unto others as they would have done unto them, not as you would have done unto you.*

In other words, don't assume that other people want to be treated the way you want to be treated. Sometimes, nothing could be further from the truth. If you like fried Mopani worms with your beer, don't assume everyone else does. One of the biggest mistakes that we can make is to think that our likes and dislikes are the other person's likes and dislikes. Everyone is different.

In a culturally diverse country, if you want to build Rapport, be guided by your Customer. If you don't see eye to eye, it may be a relationship of mutual respect. It doesn't matter how you feel. What matters is how you make others feel. Get uncomfortable.

In almost all the books on selling and service coming out of Europe and America, we are taught to look people directly in the eyes as we speak to them. We are told to sustain eye contact because it signals interest, confidence and integrity. However, in Black culture, according to Eric Molobi, it can be just the opposite. Often, when a Black South African is speaking to someone he respects, he will not look at him in the eye – because that's his sign of respect. So if you are speaking to someone and you don't connect eye to eye, don't misinterpret it as a sign of shiftiness or uncertainty. This person may simply be showing you how much he respects you.

There is another key difference between the way White and Black South Africans greet each other, and that's touch. When Blacks greet each other, there's lots of touch and hugging. As Eric says, "Physical contact is important. It means that you're a friend; you've arrived. I am close to you. We hug. It's an important sign of acceptance. Watch the way Black politicians greet those people they believe are close to them, invariably it's a hug." In White culture, it's almost the opposite. In White culture, even as we shake hands, we half pull away because we don't want to get too close.

Eric goes on to tell us an amusing story of an incident where he greeted a White associate in a large insurance company by hugging him in front of his colleagues. It was the first time this associate's White colleagues had ever met Eric and they looked on in disbelief. During a break in the meeting, one of them approached Eric and asked him what the "hug" was all about. Eric told him that it signaled that this associate is a friend and that between friends there are no barriers. Friends are close – emotionally and physically.

So what's the moral of the story? Do what you have to do to get close to the other person – even if it initially makes you feel uncomfortable. Remember the Gillis-Lipkin Ultimate Law of Rapport:

> *It doesn't matter how you feel. What matters is how you make others feel.*

In Mike's seminars, he often gets his delegates to stand up and shout: "YES! YES! YES!" at the top of their voices. He watches them as they do it. They are a little anxious and very self-conscious. Some delegates do it with gusto and others do it hesitantly and softly. After the delegates have sat down, Mike asks how many of them felt awkward doing what they've just done. About 70% raise their hands. When he asks why, they respond as follows:

I've never done it before.
I was worried what other people would think.
It feels strange.
I wasn't sure how to do it.
Adults don't behave this way.
It's not right to show your emotions in public.
I was scared that I would be the only one.
I was uncomfortable doing it.

Well, let us ask you right now: over the next twelve months, are you going to have to do things that you've never done before? Are you going to have to do things that you're not sure how to do? Are you going to have to interact with people who come from a very different culture to you? Are you going to have to do things that make you feel uncomfortable?

Of course, the answer to all these questions is "YES!" So get used to being uncomfortable. And get used to doing what's necessary to make the other person feel comfortable. Like anything else, it becomes easier and easier the more you do it.

Eight Ways to build Rapport (or apply the Juiced! Rule of Spectacular Customer Service).

If we said to you that we would give you eight powerful ways to connect deeply and instantly with your Customers, would you agree that it could prove extremely valuable for you? We can see you nodding. Read on. . .

1. **Mirror and match the way your Customer stands, sits and talks.** Here's what we mean: imitate your Customer's posture and way of speaking in a subtle way. Ensure that you reflect your Customer's behaviour. So if your Prospect talks fast and loud, then talk fast and loud. If your Prospect talks softly and slowly, then do the same. If your Customer appears tired, then stand or sit in

a tired way so you show your empathy for the Customer's state. Then verbalize your empathy and lift the Customer up. For example, "Hmm, looks like you've had a tough day, huh? Well, the good news is that it's almost over."

2. **Use the language your Customer uses.** Listen to the words your Customer uses and build them into your vocabulary. Listen especially carefully to those words that the Customer uses when he is excited or happy. Just by using these words, you will trigger your Customer's feelings of joy and affection for you. Think about how you feel when someone uses words that you love and relate to. Here are some examples of how we build Rapport with our Customers:

   When we are with Customers in the Restaurant industry: "We have some sizzling ideas for you. They will make your mouths water."

   When we are with Customers in the Automotive industry: "We need to overhaul our approach so that we can fire on all cylinders. We'll get your motor running."

   When we are with Customers in the Financial industry: "We need to make more emotional deposits into the relationships with our Customers. The ROE, Return on Emotion, will be extremely high and that's the bottom line."

3. **Pay your Customers sincere compliments wherever and whenever you can.** We have written a lot about compliments in this book. But please notice the emphasis on the word "sincere". Nothing will turn off a Customer faster than a false compliment. So from today, make sure that you pay people at least ten sincere compliments a day.

4. **Practise the OMO Principle: give your Customers referrals, especially from people in their industry.** Have you seen those OMO washing powder commercials? Why do you think they have made OMO the number one selling brand of washing powder in South Africa? Referrals. The commercials feature ordinary, everyday consumers who tell viewers how effective OMO is in their lives. They are believable and credible.

   Ask yourself how you can apply the OMO principle in your life. Giving your Customers referrals from people in their industries accelerates the process of Rapport enormously. A referral immediately allows you to tell the Customer how you handled similar challenges to the one facing the Customer. Remember, it's all about trust, and the faster you can get someone's trust, the sooner they will commit to you.

5. **Listen with your Third Ear.** *"As you go through life, you are going to have many opportunities to keep your mouth shut. Take advantage of all of them." James Dent*
   One of the most powerful ways to generate Rapport is simply to listen with genuine interest to the Customer. We all love to be with people who make us feel special. The most powerful way to make people feel special is to listen to them intensely. Dr Bernard Levinson calls it "listening with your Third Ear". That's when you listen with your sixth sense. You concentrate all your energy on the Customer. You listen with your heart. You listen for the meaning between the words. You listen to the silences. You listen to the gestures. You listen to the expressions. By your listening, you are saying to the Customer, "What you have to say to me is so important, I don't want to miss even a word."

   Examine your own ability to listen. When people speak to you, do you find your mind wandering? Do you fiddle with things around you? Are you trying to do something else while people are talking to you? What kind of expression do you have on your face? What does your body language say? If all you do as a result of reading this book is build your listening skills, you will deliver Spectacular Customer Service.

Always make notes when a Customer is talking to you. Nothing communicates your interest and commitment more than actually writing down what the Customer is saying. Taking notes tells the Customer that you are going to follow up what's being said and take action.

Never put square pegs in round holes: When Protea Hotels go and see a Prospect about hosting their conference, they have the ability to force-fit a Customer into an hotel or resort that might not be optimal for the Customer's needs. It may suit Protea to do it because they may have a vacant facility at the time that they wish to hire out. However Protea know that if they do this, they may get the conference from the Customer on this occasion but they will never get any more business from her again.

Instead, the Protea Hotels team listen very carefully to the Customer. They make sure they understand what the Customer really wants and then they put a square peg into a square hole – even if it means recommending a competitor's facility if Protea Hotels do not have anything suitable.

6. Bring up a subject of mutual interest. Talk about those things that interest the Customer. If you are familiar with the Customer's business, talk about it. If not, find out about it. Or just ask intelligent questions about the Customer's business. However, if you are prepared to do your homework, you will greatly impress the Customer because so few people are prepared to invest just a little bit of extra time in knowing their Customers. Or ask about the Customer's personal interests and build the conversation around them. The moment you talk about mutual interests, you accelerate the process of building Rapport.

7. **Use humour.** We've spoken a lot about humour in this book. We'd like to add just three new words here: experiment, test, practise. Experiment with new approaches, test their ability to make people smile and then practise your humour until you become a master. Both of us use humour as a key tool in our interactions with others. We are constantly trying new approaches, testing them and discarding what no longer works.

8. **Understand your Customers' beliefs and values.** Unless you understand why your Customers do what they do, how can you truly connect with them? A very simple way of getting a sense of Customers' beliefs and values is to ask them two basic questions:

    - When it comes to. . ., what is most important to you? (The blank refers to whatever subject you're discussing). When a Customer tells you what's most important to them, they're telling you about their beliefs and values. Listen carefully and ensure you reflect these beliefs and values in the way you deal with them. For example, if someone tells you that staying fit is very important to them, you know that you should weave health and wellbeing into your presentation or interaction with this person.

    - What has to happen for you feel as though your expectations have been met? This simple question will help you understand the Customer's rules for satisfaction, not yours. For example, recently, Mike was briefed by a Customer on a workshop she wanted him to hold with her people. He asked her, "What has to happen for you to feel that my talk is a success?" She responded by saying, "Firstly, they must be incredibly motivated. Secondly, they must have specific tools that they can go out and use immediately." By asking this simple question, Mike understood how he would be evaluated. What's more, the Customer felt pleased because Mike helped her communicate what she truly wanted.

Now that you have the Eight Ways to build Rapport, go and apply them today. And let us know how they're working by visiting www.mikelipkin.com or fax us on (011) 728-6907.

Now let's look at two highly successful companies that apply Empathy and Rapport to connect deeply with their Customers at the expense of their competition:

Empathy, Rapport, Intimacy - no-one does it better than Estee Lauder and her son, Leonard. And that's why women find Lauder mesmerizing - (Fortune 25 May 1998).

The following article is an excerpt from the story on Estee Lauder which we discovered in the Fortune magazine online archives. We are deeply grateful to Fortune because the following words are a superb description of the power of rapport and intimacy. The more technologically driven the world becomes, the more people crave human contact and touch. However, as you will read, reaching out and touching people takes commitment, effort and airmiles. Very few people are prepared to make this investment. But for those who do, the rewards are huge. Estee Lauder is one of the most successful cosmetics companies in the world because they religiously apply empathy, rapport and intimacy in their dealings with Customers. Enjoy the story:

Leonard Lauder has recognized that cosmetics are

personal, intimate; that increasingly the trend is toward specialization, towards brands that make a woman feel she's buying something that's made just for her, that conforms to her unique style, her "very special" look. Leonard Lauder's goal is to own not one single brand with mass appeal but instead a collection of dozens and dozens of brands, each targeting a different kind of Customer.

Bobbi Brown, of Estee Lauder's Bobbi Brown Essentials line, praises Lauder in these terms: "When Leonard gives speeches, he talks about his close relationships with people, and everyone in the room thinks he's talking just about them." Touching people, becoming intimate with Customers, charming everyone he comes into contact with – no one does it better than Leonard.

At Estee Lauder headquarters in Manhattan's General Motors Building, at the elevators, next to the entrances, you'll find little frosted squares of pale green glass engraved with a motto: *Bringing the best to everyone we touch.* That motivational clichè is to be interpreted literally. Estee Lauder herself understood that selling cosmetics works best if you can get intimate with the Customer. Intimacy means not groping but touching – lightly placing three fingers on someone's forehead, smoothing lotions on her cheeks, applying gloss to her lips.

Like his mother before him, Leonard Lauder knows that business is about relationships. It's about making people feel important. He travels compulsively, greeting the women who sell his makeup, checking up on cosmetic counters everywhere. Last year, he racked up 165 000 airmiles, which is about equal to travelling around the world six and a half times. "I'm in department stores all the time. You know, probably no one travels the way I do," he says, "You speak to retailers around the world; no one else visits them. I am the only person in the cosmetics industry that the retailers around the world know. Because my competitors don't care. I care, personally. If you asked me what would I like to do on my vacation, I'd say, I'd like to go and visit stores." Touching people, building relationships, is a sales technique that Leonard Lauder expects every person in his company to perfect.

One of Leonard Lauder's sales techniques must be the oldest in the book: within 24 hours or so of meeting someone, he invariably writes that person an intimate, often handwritten note. In fact, he's famous for his notes, for his ability to always say just the right thing and to touch people just that way.

We have taken a leaf out of Leonard Lauder's book in the way we have marketed this book. It is being produced through our publishing company, Touch The Sky (Pty) Ltd. We have also entered into a unique agreement with the CNA whereby they are the exclusive retailers of this book. We invest a massive amount of time visiting CNA stores across the country and talking to retail staff. Mike even gives motivational talks to the staff countrywide so they can sell not only his book but all the merchandise in the store. We want to be seen as a powerful resource by the CNA. They are as much a part of this book's success as the words you are reading now.

How Dell Computers makes the little guys feel big (Forbes April 17 2000). **Lesson: treat small businesses like the big business that they are.**

"Dell knows something that other guys just aren't getting yet," says Keith Dellova, Vice President of Technology at Onsite Trading Inc, a brokerage firm that buys all its gear from Dell. Which is this: if you want to win the hearts (and wallets) of small business Customers, you need to make them feel important. That mantra has helped Dell become number one among PC makers in the U.S. small business market. Dell's sales to home and small business Customers grew 70% last year. Over the past three years, Dell has built liaisons with thousands of small business Customers, using a team of about 250 "relationship sales reps".

Dellova talks every day with his Dell Account Manager, Jacqueline Godlewski. And not just about computers. She knows about his parrots. He knows about her dogs. "Jackie," he says, "is my adopted sister." That's what we call Rapport!

Of course, Dell also offer their small Customers tangible reasons for their business. Not only do they get a dedicated account rep, but they also get an array of special services – like the customized "Premier Page" that lets them place orders on the Web and keep track of what they've bought. They also get access to the Dell Plus programme, in which company technicians preload their computers with any software they want, including their own company's customized applications. Dell also frequently flies small business Customers to Texas for a tour of its plant and to meet with executives.

Interestingly, and this is another reason why we've included this excellent article in this book, Jacqueline Godlewski joined Dell in 1998 after ten years in the hotel and hospitality industry. She believes that it was good training for selling computers. As Godlewski states, "My goal is to make sure that every Customer looks forward to calling me!" Do yours?

If there's one lesson this article has for all large South African businesses, it's this: Treat small businesses like the big business that they are. This country's future depends not on the top 200 publicly listed companies but on the thousands of small businesses that are testing their entrepreneurial mettle in the marketplace. As Dell has demonstrated, it can be very, very lucrative.

Deepen your involvement with your Customers. The more time you spend with them, the higher your Empathy and Rapport levels will be. If you want more business, hunt in packs.

We've shared our insights with you about how you can get closer to your Customers so that they increase both their trust and the amount of money they spend with you. However, there is one truth which is so basic that even we got it first time: *If you want to get closer to your Customers, get them to spend more time with you.* The smart retailers really understand this fact. That's why, as you may have noticed, stores are being redesigned to intrigue and entice you to stay a little longer. There is a direct correlation between the amount of time someone spends in a store and the amount of money they spend there.

Henry Barenblatt, CEO of Research Surveys – South Africa's largest consumer market research company, understands the power of deepening Customer contact and involvement. "The average research project takes ten weeks." he says. "Once the project has been approved, the person who commissions the project doesn't expect to hear from Research Surveys until it's time for presentation – because that's the norm in the industry. However, our research executives call the Customer every week to tell her about our progress, problems and solutions. We believe involving the Customer in this manner is vital."

Barenblatt continues, "Research Surveys involve the Customer deeply right at the beginning as well. Customers are invited to come into the company and meet all the players on the team, from the field staff to the people who do the processing of the data to the Customer Service executives. By the time the briefing is finished, the Customer is intimately aware of the people and the challenges involved. We also take the Customers into the field so that they can see the project being implemented. Research Surveys is an open house. Our Customers can observe any part of the process at any time. It does take a little more time. But it's more than worth it."

What we like about Research Surveys is that they also hunt in packs. The team takes the brief, not the individual. They therefore have both the perspective of a group of people as well as a broader level of contact with the Customer from the beginning of the relationship.

And here's the kicker: Research Surveys didn't achieve market leadership through discounting. They are not even on par with the competition in terms of their pricing. Research Surveys sell their services at a healthy 20% premium relative to the competition. They are honest and transparent with their Customers. In research, the integrity of the information is vital. Customers know they're paying more, but the trust that they've invested in Research Surveys makes it worthwhile. Makes you think, doesn't it?

"No matter how brilliant we think we are, we are all fools at some stage or another." Reg Lascaris

If you want to deliver Spectacular Customer Service, you have to suffer fools gladly. People who are intolerant will never be successful. In fact, intelligence without tolerance is not only useless, it's downright destructive. Intolerance breeds a whole range of other undermining forces like impatience, prejudice, narrow-mindedness, anger, irritation, agitation, rudeness, frustration, disrespect, discourtesy, impoliteness and insensitivity. And that's just for starters.

What is a fool anyway? Well, have you noticed that a fool is anyone who doesn't see things the way that you do? Or a fool is anyone who disagrees with you. Or a fool is anyone who makes your life more difficult. Well, from this moment on, beware of calling anyone a fool or even thinking of someone as a fool. Just thinking about someone in a negative light will rob you of your ability to serve them. You know why? Because thoughts are real. Your thoughts are the energy you radiate towards everyone around you. Think of the last time you thought negatively of someone while they were in front of you. Couldn't they feel it? Didn't you talk, look and stand in a negative way? And didn't the other person reciprocate your antagonism. Remember, other people are mirrors that reflect back at you what you are.

So before you even begin to think of the other person as the fool, ask yourself whether it's not you who is the fool. Are you behaving like a champion or a chump? Are you in control of your emotions or are they in control of you? Aren't you supposed to be the leader in this situation? Are you acting like one? Are you stepping up and taking yourself to the next level? Or are you doing something that you're definitely going to regret later on?

Here's the core quality of Spectacular Customer Service Champions: they are driven by the passion to serve. They never judge the people they're serving. They know that the greater the challenge presented to them by the Customer, the better they will become as a service provider. They genuinely want to help the Customer resolve her problem. And because they go into the situation with an attitude of service and contribution, tolerance, courtesy and patience automatically follow. Ask not what your Customers can do for you. Ask what you can do for your Customers.

Install CCTV in your brain. Be conscious of yourself but don't be self-conscious.

Have you ever looked back at a situation and wished you could have handled it in a different way? Haven't there been times when you thought of the best words to say to a Customer after the event had passed? Have you ever felt embarrassed or angry with yourself because of how you behaved in a situation? You know what? We all have. The challenge is how to minimize those occurrences so that we act in the best way when we need to.

Well, we have just the system to help you be your best whenever you need to. It's called "Mental CCTV". And it works just like the closed circuit TV cameras you see in stores and buildings all around you, except that this CCTV is in your head. It's the camera that observes you in whatever you're doing. The outstanding achievers have the ability to watch themselves in action and adjust their behaviour accordingly. Try this: in your next encounter with a Customer, pretend that you are watching yourself on TV. Would you like what you see? Would you smile at the way you are handling the Customer? Would you want to see more? Or would you want to turn it off?

The best of the best have the ability to see themselves in action and adjust their delivery before anyone else tells them to. They know that their mission is to reward their Customers for the privilege of doing business with them. They make the experience pleasurable for the Customer. They are conscious of how they are performing but they are not inhibited in their performance. Most importantly, they turn on their CCTV in the most intense, heated moments. Their CCTV helps them avoid the outbursts or comments that can lead to regret later. Make sure you become one of these outstanding performers today. Install Mental CCTV. It's free but it will make you rich and famous.

Customers are won or lost one Customer at a time: Chunk Down. If you don't, the pressure is going to kill you. Treat every Customer as though they're your only Customer and you'll make all your Customers very happy.

When are most the problems with Customer Service likely to occur – during off-peak periods or during peak periods?

Obviously during the peak periods. It's easy to deliver Spectacular Service when there's no pressure. It's when the heat is on that people tend to burn out. We see it all the time. We see it at the airports, the hotels, the restaurants, the stores, the call centres and so on. As the pressure builds, we become more and more anxious. We see the line of Customers in front of us, or we think about how many Customers are on hold, or we think about all the calls we still need to return and we get more and more uptight. You know the feeling: the tightness in your chest, the lead ball in your stomach, the sweat on your palms, the physical tension throughout your body. It's hell. And you can't serve anyone effectively in that state. Your Customers will feel your discomfort as acutely as you do.

So Chunk Down. That means simply that you can only deal with one Customer at a time. So when you're dealing with that Customer, concentrate only on that Customer. Don't worry about anything or anyone else. Look into his eyes. Let him know that he is the most important person in the world to you at that moment. Speak to him with deep affection and respect in your voice. He'll feel it and he'll respond. If you handle this Customer extremely well, you'll take care of all the other Customers as well. But if you mishandle this Customer, what happens to the way you handle all the Customers after him? Yup, you mess them all up. You know why? Because you carry the frustration and negativity over into the next encounter and the next and the next. Before you know it, you've had a really lousy day. So you go home and take it out on your family. You make them unhappy. So you have a couple of drinks and stew over what happened. Then you go to bed upset. You wake up the next morning in a bad mood. You really don't look forward to going to work. And the whole cycle begins again. Well, know this: you can interrupt the entire negative pattern simply by handling your next Customer magnificently. Come on, try it out. Treat every

Customer as though he is your only Customer and you'll make all your Customers very happy.

Stephen Stills expressed this concept beautifully in his famous song, "Love the One You're With":

If you're down and confused
And you don't remember who you're talkin' to
Concentration slips away
'Cause your baby is so far away
Well, there's a rose in the fisted glove
And the eagle flies with the dove.
And if you can't be with the one you love,
Love the one you're with
Love the one you're with.

Practise loving the one you're with right now, no matter where you are. Make whoever is in front of you a loved one. Make him or her the only person in your life just for this moment. Concentrate on making his experience with you the best thing that will happen to him this week. And then do it with the next person and the next and the next. . .The only moment you can manage is this moment right now. So make it a magic moment and help others do the same.

Ngiyakubona – I see You.

Ngiyakubona is a Zulu word that means literally "I see you". But, according to Jimmy Ntintili, it really means I see past your appearance. I see past the fact that you may black or white, poor or rich, a man or a woman. I see the best part of you. I see your soul. I honourably acknowledge your presence as an equal. I do not judge you. I am open to you. I embrace you. I welcome you. I share my warmth and my spirit with you. I serve you not because of what you're going to give me. I serve you because I want to serve You. You receive the emphasis, not me. My role is to make you happy. And if you're happy, then I'm happy.

Eric Molobi, Chairman of Kagiso, regards the Spirit of Ngiyakubona as the highest form of integrity. He says,

> *"I value integrity profoundly. I never approach life with an agenda that the other person is wrong and I'm right. Therefore, when it comes to service, you need to have integrity. By that I mean when you look at a Prospect, treat him or her equally. Don't pay more attention to a beautiful young woman than you would to an old man, or to a wealthy looking person than to a person who looks like they have less money. Say to yourself, "Here comes a human being. I have to ensure that I treat this human being with dignity and respect. He is a person just like me. I will not ignore him. I will put him at ease. I will relate to him with compassion and conscience. I'll do it right. I'm not in a hurry. I'll make a difference in his life."*

We believe Molobi's words define the spirit of the entire book – the spirit of Customer Service as an expression of compassion and contribution. In fact, all over the world, the true Customer Service Champions apply the Spirit of Ngiyakubona, whether they know it or not. It's not the money that truly drives them. It's their compassion, generosity and caring. It's the pleasure they get from giving people pleasure. And this motivation applies as much to financial consultants as it does to IT vendors as it does to hoteliers.

Beware of "The Look." It is the precise opposite of Ngiyakubona. And, contrary to popular belief, Looks can kill.

Are you practicing the Spirit of Ngiyakubona? What is the primary motivation that drives you to serve your Customers? When a Customer looks into your eyes, what does he see? Empathy and caring? Or impatience, apathy and judgement? Remember, you don't have to say a single word for people to know exactly what you think. Just like us, we know that at one time or another you've received "The Look" from others. What's "The Look"? It's that expression of boredom, contempt, annoyance, anger or irritation on others' faces when they don't want to be doing what they're forced to do. "The Look" is the precise opposite of Ngiyakubona. It belittles and humiliates others. Just one "Look" is all it takes to kill a Customer relationship. We hope you never give it to another person again.

Ngiyakubona in action: How Protea served the South African National Council for the Blind (SANCB). The simple, ultimate Customer Service test: do your Customers think of you as their friend?

At the end of 1999, one of the Protea Hotels hosted a conference for the Blind. As always, Protea met with the Customer beforehand to prepare themselves for the conference. However what really impressed Dr William Rowland, Executive Director of the SANCB, was Protea's Spirit of Ngiyakubona. His letter said it all:

> *Dear Friends*
>
> *I begin this letter by calling you "Dear Friends" because that is the way I feel about the relationship which developed between our conference delegates and yourselves. It was clear that the hotel staff had been well prepared for our visit, but over and above this, you also gave your personal commitment to meeting all of our needs.*
>
> *Please know that your courtesy, service and friendliness was deeply appreciated. Your assistance to blind Guests was particularly valued.*
>
> *Yours truly*
>
> *William Rowland*

As Rowland writes, the Spirit of Ngiyakubona really means turning Customers into friends. It's when the relationship ceases to be about business and becomes one of people joined together by common values, affection and commitment to each other.

Let us ask you, have you ever received a letter like the one William sent to Protea? We know you have. How did that make you feel? How did it make your staff feel? Proud? Fulfilled? Motivated? Appreciated? Or all of the above?

Letters like the one featured above are the highest prize in Customer Service. They are a step beyond even Gold Medal status because they are sent from the heart. They are an expression of thanks from a grateful person. They're also a reminder that people will forget what you said. They will forget what you did. But people will never forget how you made them feel. Here's the simple, ultimate test of Spectacular Customer Service:

Do your Customers think of you as their friend?

The Pavlov's Dog Guide to Spectacular Customer Service. It's all about the pleasure motive. Whether you're an accountant, an advisor, an adman or an actor, you're really in show business. Have you heard of a scientist called Ivan Pavlov? He lived over 60 years ago and he discovered the meaning of the word "conditioning." This is what he did: he fed a dog and every time he fed the dog, he rang a bell. After three days, he asked the dog what it was eating and the dog replied, "I don't know but its name rings a bell." Seriously, what do you think the dog did every time it heard the bell, even when there was no food? Obviously, it salivated. Well here's our question for you,

When Customers think of you, do they salivate?

This is a serious question. In fact, it could be the most serious question in the entire book. You know why? Because the two primal forces that drive all human beings are the need to avoid pain and the desire to get pleasure. If the Customer is indifferent towards you, or if he associates you with any kind of discomfort, he will avoid you and you will starve. However, if your name triggers the Customer's pleasure sensations, he will come back again and again. So how much of a pleasure are you making it for your Customers to deal with you? Are you designing a specific approach to serving your Customers that makes them feel outstanding? Does the mere mention of your name motivate your Customer to shout "YES" at the top of her voice?

Whether you're an accountant, an advisor, an adman or an actor, you're really in show business. Your mission is to interest, entertain and stimulate your Customers while you serve them. We promise you that *the actual experience of dealing with you is as important as the actual product or service you are selling.* Look around you: the people who Juice their Customers with showmanship and stage management are far more successful than those who don't. Investec Bank is a classic example. They even went to the massive effort and expense of bringing Larry King to South Africa just so they could introduce him to their Customers. What's more, their Customers loved it. The press reported that many people became Customers of Investec just so they could meet King. Crazy but true.

Many South Africans have been brought up in homes where we were taught that children should be seen and not heard. This "keep quiet" culture stays with us our entire lives. As a result, we're a nation that is not used to standing up and standing out. We don't naturally take to the notion of entertaining and stimulating our Customers by doing the unusual and the extraordinary. Well, we're advising you: if you want to be successful in the future, begin now. All it takes is a bit of imagination and ingenuity. The Americans do this extremely well. They're flooding into South Africa. And if you don't captivate your Customers, they will.

Even beggars need to establish Rapport and make you smile: "It's for you. . ."

You'll love this story. It could only happen in South Africa. It's about a beggar who understands Rapport and Spectacular Customer Service as well as any business school graduate.

Every motorist in this country has been pestered by the thousands of beggars standing at traffic lights with cardboard signs that read, "No Job. Need Food. Please help. God bless you." In fact, they've become so numerous that most of us don't even take notice of them anymore. Well, what do you do if you are forced to stand on street corners and beg? 99.9% of these unfortunate souls just stand here and hope that a charitable motorist will stop at their traffic light.

One man, though, understands the meaning of entertainment and differentiation. He understands how to create instant Empathy and Rapport. We met him at the corner of Grayston and Catherine Avenues in Sandton at 17h00 during peak hour traffic. His only presentation equipment was a discarded telephone, his voice, his creativity and his own exuberance. As we stopped at the traffic lights, he approached our car. He pursed his lips together and out came the perfect sound of a phone ringing. He picked up the receiver, looked at us, smiled broadly and handed the receiver to us with the words, "It's for you". Mike actually began reaching for the phone before he burst out laughing. Needless to say, we showered this streetwise entrepreneur with all the change we had on us.

As we inched forward, we looked back to see our hero extending his phone to the car behind us. The driver was also laughing and reaching into her purse for change. Which just goes to show firstly, that there is no such thing as a hopeless situation if you understand the meaning of differentiation and implement it with flair and confidence. And secondly, if your focus is always on the wellbeing of the Customer, in this case the donor, you will find a way to connect with her and achieve your desired results.

The Gillis-Lipkin Formula for Spectacular Customer Service Factor Three: Preparation.

Let's begin with the Seven Lessons of the Lumberjacks.

Once upon a time, in a land far away, there lived two men, Peter and Paxton. They made a living as lumberjacks. Every day they would go out into the forest and cut down as many trees as they could which they would then sell to the local community.

Peter was very hardworking. He would rise each day before dawn, pack some food and head out into the forest. There, he would work non-stop for six hours. He would then take a very short break for lunch before he continued with his arduous task until well after sunset. Eventually, he would stagger home, exhausted.

Paxton, on the other hand, didn't believe in hard work. He would rise long after Peter. In fact, by the time he passed Peter on the way to his neck of the woods, Peter was already in a state of extreme perspiration. Then Paxton would take numerous breaks followed by a long lunch which in turn was followed by a siesta. Finally, Paxton would return home while Peter was still covering himself in sawdust.

Now, although Peter was neither the curious nor the complaining sort, he couldn't help wondering how Paxton always seemed to cut down more trees than he did. He was fully aware of Paxton's shorter working hours, long breaks and siestas. He knew that Paxton didn't employ anyone else to work for him. And yet, Paxton consistently delivered a higher yield of felled trees every day.

One day, Peter could bear it no longer. As Paxton passed him on his way home, Peter shouted to him, "Hey Paxton. How the heck do you do it? You start long after me. You finish long before me. You're always taking a break and yet you always cut down more trees than me." Paxton just looked at him, smiled and shouted back, "Hey Peter, you weren't watching me closely enough. If you were, you would have noticed that I spend my entire breaks sharpening my axe."

So what are the Seven Lessons of the Lumberjacks? We believe they're simple:

Stop doing and start thinking.
Constantly prepare yourself for constant improvement.
It's not the hours you put into your work, it's the work you put into your hours.
Every action either sharpens your senses or deadens them.
Preparation is power.
Never confuse activity with progress.
Switch off your automatic pilot and switch on your opportunity radar.

Gordon Joffe, Managing Director of Polo Clothing, Cape Town, expresses these lessons well when he says, "It requires the same amount of effort to do it wrong as it does to do it right. It's just that we have been conditioned to believe that it's much more difficult to do it right. The same principle applies to being nice and courteous with Customers and colleagues versus abrupt and indifferent. It doesn't take more effort. It does take more awareness, training and practise."

Overload and battle fatigue: we're trying to do too much with too little. The Ultimate Irony: what we want more than anything else is for the people who serve us to take our stress away. And yet, the people who serve us cause us the most stress.

Wherever we go, we see people trying to do twice as much with half the resources in a quarter of the time with a fraction of the training. We see the look of desperation as people lurch from one crisis to another. We see mistakes creep into Customer Service that drive Customers mad. We see people being ambushed by problems that they should have seen coming from a mile away. We see people being overloaded with responsibilities while being bombarded with change. What's more, many Customer Service providers in South Africa are people who are still living a primal, survival-based existence. They're suffering from battle fatigue.

We know what it's like. Day in and day out, the same old routine; the same old problems, frustrations and irritations. Repetition can dull the senses and rob us of our motivation. Tiredness is the great enemy of great service. We click into automatic pilot and habit takes over. Our voice becomes a monotone. We move like a machine and we sound like one too. All we can think about is finishing time or Friday or the next holiday.

Whether we sell insurance, shoes or skiing holidays, it's easy to become jaded. It's easy to lose our passion and our love for what we're doing. As Customers of other people, we see it all the time. We see it in people's eyes. We see it in their expressions. We see it in the way they walk and talk. It's called tiredness. Tiredness not just of the mind or even of the body. It's tiredness of the spirit. It's when we lose our love for what we're doing and just go through the motions. Does this ring a bell with you? Are you a dead person walking or are you one of the fabulous few who sustain their spring and passion when all others have lost theirs? Are you a role model who is committed to making your Customers happy each and every day, or are you just another robot who is barely complying with his job description?

Customers are being forced to deal with people who are stressed out of their minds. And that's the Ultimate Irony: what we want more than anything else is for the people who serve us to take our stress away. And yet, the people who serve us cause us the most stress.

Customers are crying out: "Please take away my hassles. Please simplify my life. Please help me concentrate on what's really important to me. Do my thinking for me so that I don't have to. Please be the one factor in my life that is reliable. Everything is crumbling and changing around me. I'm running faster and harder just to keep it all together. Help me Rhonda! Help, help me Rhonda! Help me if you can!"

Except, here's the multi-headed problem: how can I help you if I'm not even sure what it is I should be doing for you? How can I help you if I'm not even sure what the ultimate benefit is that I'm giving you? How can I help you if I'm not even sure what I should be saying to you? How can I help you if I'm not even sure what I should be focusing on? How can I help you if I am scared out of my mind? Read on dear Reader and let's see if we have any answers for you. . .

Don't confuse the means with the end. You're not selling Service, you're selling States.

In our shows across the country, we ask people what it is that they really give their Clients. They tell us service, care, value for money, affordability, reliability, partnership, solutions and so on. But aren't all those elements really a means to an end? If so, what is the end in mind we're talking about?

Well, let's take this book for example. We're not just helping you to improve your level of service, communication or people skills. Those are the means to an end. Our end in mind is to excite you and put you in a permanently Juiced state. It is to make you successful, happy and a force for good. It is to help you become the kind of person who influences hundreds of other people to take themselves to the next level. That's why the tone is so upbeat. That's why we've designed it so that you instantly "get it" without having to think too hard or too long about what we're saying.

So we're in the "Get You Juiced!" business. What business are you really in? What is the "end-state" you want to put people in? As you think about these questions, revisit the module on "Purpose".

For you, it's your job. For him, it's his honeymoon. Are you making it magic or tragic?

Let us ask you this question: have you ever had a really special moment ruined because the person who served you didn't care about your big occasion? Or have you ever been annoyed with someone because they didn't treat you and your Guest with the respect and attention you felt you deserved? Often, right? But how many times have you been guilty of exactly the same sin with the Customers who you serve?

Here's an extreme, genuine example of the "Magic or Tragic Phenomenon." Only names and places have been changed to protect guilty people:

The Story of Jan and Juanita.

Jan is a 27-year-old mechanic who began working at Lombard's Bakkies (pick-up trucks) in Agies, Northern Province, when he was 16 years old. Today he is a partner in the business. He is a hard-working, highly committed professional who lives modestly and has managed to save a third of his income every month. Recently, Jan went to a party at his third cousin's house where he met Juanita, a 23-year-old dark-eyed beauty with a body that makes grown men cry.

Juanita, however, is also a clever and experienced businesswoman who runs a highly successful network marketing company. When Jan and Juanita saw each other, friends say that the electricity between them was visible, even under the fluorescent lights of the mobile disco.

It took only three months for Jan and Juanita to decide to marry, have kids and live the good life – blue sky, bucks, braaivleis and bakkies. They were married by the local Dominee in a small but charming ceremony at the Agies Chapel in Hoof-Straat. For their honeymoon, Jan decided to splurge for the first time in his entire life: for their honeymoon, he took his young bride to the Umhlanga Centennial Ocean Plaza, a well known three-star resort.

Jan was breathless with excitement as he opened the bakkie door for Juanita and escorted her into the lobby of Umhlanga Centennial Ocean Plaza. This was the highlight of his young life. He had spent ten hours a day, six days a week for the past twelve years, looking into the bowels of bakkies. He had swallowed grease, oil and radiator fluid as he stared into the belly of the iron beasts he healed everyday. But, thought Jan, it was all worth it for this moment: the first day of his honeymoon with Juanita, his bride, his light, his everything.

As Jan and Juanita approached the check-in counter, a young woman, Claudia, stood in front of a computer, speaking on the phone. She appeared to be hassled as she tried to resolve a problem that the Guest in Chalet 23 had with the airconditioner in his room. Her lips tightened and whitened as she assured the Guest that the maintenance man would be there within the hour. Meanwhile Jan and Juanita stood there, waiting patiently. Eventually, Claudia put the phone down. Jan began to speak but Claudia held up her hand indicating that she had to go into the back office to get hold of the maintenance man.

And still Jan and Juanita stood patiently and waited. Despite himself, Jan felt his mood begin to deflate. When Claudia returned five minutes later, she greeted the couple with her standard "Welcome to the Umhlanga Centennial Ocean Plaza. Can I help you?" She still seemed upset from her previous experience. Jan felt as though the last thing she wanted to do was serve him. But at least she was efficient. Within minutes, she had checked Jan and Juanita into their twin-bedded chalet. However, although Jan had told the resort that this was his honeymoon, Claudia made no mention of this fact. A porter took their bags to the room and left. For a few moments, Jan and Juanita faced each other, overcome with a sense of anticlimax. This was supposed to be the most special moment of their lives and yet they both felt strangely flat.

This story, however, has a happy ending. The weather obliged. The beach was clean. The water was warm. Their love for each other was strong. They had a good time. And, at the time of writing, Juanita is expecting their first child – conceived that very week.

Why did we tell you this story?

Claudia complied with the rules of her job. She checked in Jan and Juanita and sorted out the problem with the airconditioner in Chalet 23 efficiently. So what's the problem? Well, did Claudia really act with both her heart and her head? Did she empathize with the honeymoon couple? Did she make their check-in a marvellous experience? Did she help them celebrate the start of the most enjoyable week of their lives? Did she truly know what benefit she was supposed to give to Juan and Jaunita? The answer to all these questions is obviously a big, fat NO! You see, for Claudia, Jan and Juanita were just two of the thousands of people she checks in every month. But for Jan and Juanita, this was the first and only time they had ever checked in anywhere as a couple. It wasn't just their honeymoon, it was their fantasy come true. That is, until Claudia messed it up for them.

Why didn't Claudia act with more emotion? Was it her fault? Was she trained correctly? Did the booking form indicate that Jan and Juanita were a honeymoon couple? Was Claudia merely in a bad mood that day because of all the pressure on her? Who knows? And who cares? Not the Customer. The Customer is only concerned about the attitude and competence with which she is treated. These are the "Visibles". The "Invisibles" are all the actions behind the scene to make the Visibles happen.

What should have happened that day? Claudia could have smiled. She could have welcomed the couple and congratulated them. She could have made a big deal about the honeymoon suite they were getting. She could have called the manager to add his greetings to the special occasion. There could have been a bottle of champagne, in a bucket of ice, in the room. . .

We're sure that you agree with us: all of these initiatives are not revolutionary. They do not require a lot of brainpower or technical innovation. So what would you have done to make Juan and Juanita very happy from the moment they stepped into the Umhlanga Centennial Ocean Plaza? How would you have prepared Claudia and her colleagues to provide the Honeymoon couple with Spectacular Service? What kind of system, culture, leadership and training do you think is required?

Step up and stand guard at the door of your mind. You are the CEO of your own career. If you fail to prepare, you prepare to fail. The head must govern the heart: how big a priority is Customer Service really in your company?

We've given you the first two factors of the formula for Spectacular Customer Service – Desire and Empathy. And, like any good formula, you have to know what factors to put in first. Well, both Desire and Empathy precede Preparation because without those two emotions, nothing else can happen. They are the heart of Spectacular Customer Service. But the head must govern the heart. Customer Service must be a massive priority.

Everyone must be in constant preparation for the next level of service delivery. It must begin with the top person and filter all the way to the rockface. Then it must be recycled all the way back to the top person, beginning with frontline staff. Preparation for consistently improving Customer Service is not the responsibility of somebody else. It's the responsibility of everyone. In the best service companies, some of the best ideas come from the frontline where people go belly to belly with the Customer.

So take action today. Look around you. See what you can improve and do it. Talk to the people around you about your ideas. Of course some people will be negative and unresponsive, but keep on keeping on. Stand guard at the door of your mind and help others do the same. Talk to your colleagues about some of the ideas you've picked up in this book. Throw them around. Discard what doesn't work and apply what does.

When we ask you to "Step up", we're really asking you to act like you own the company. Seriously, if it was all your money tied up in the business and you were the beneficiary of all the profits, what would you do? What changes would you make? How would you prepare the enterprise to take itself to the next level?

Well, know this, you are the CEO of your own career. Your actions today will determine your future tomorrow. If you act like you're just a paid wage earner, you'll stay just a wage earner. No-one else is going to lead you by the hand to fame and fortune. As the Business Times reported recently, "You're on your own in the new job world". So see every Customer as your personal asset. See them as your ticket to ultimate success. Begin preparing today for the next "You". Ultimately, no matter who you're working for, you are building the company called You (Pty) Ltd.

If you fail to prepare yourself for your career, you prepare to fail in your career. And you know what? Most South Africans haven't even thought about what we're discussing with you here. They've left their success to chance. They think that luck, the lottery or hard work alone will get them to the top. But, as we've learnt from Peter and Paxton, that's a myth. In fact, if you keep your nose close to the grindstone, all that's going to happen is that you're going to end up with a short nose.

When it comes to Customer Service, most South African companies talk the talk but they don't walk the walk.

Based on Rands and Cents invested, what's the importance that South African companies place on Customer Service? Not a heck of a lot. After working with over 250 Blue Chip companies in South Africa, Henry Barenblatt, CEO of Research Surveys, believes that companies tend to specialize in technical training. They want an immediate jump in productivity so their training funds are primarily spent on enhancing task-specific competency.

Very few companies spend any real time and effort in focusing on delivering Spectacular Service. Barenblatt believes that a maximum of ten percent of South African companies invest substantially in Customer Service training or research. And yet, that's where the real competitive opportunity resides. As we've already shown, there is a direct correlation between Spectacular Customer Service and Customer attitudes towards the company. We believe strongly that, as a result of this book, if you invest massively in enhancing your quality of service, you will achieve huge success in the marketplace.

We must caution you, however, that Spectacular Customer Service is not a get-rich-quick fix. There's no easy walk to Spectacular Service. Yes, it is easy to get Juiced! for a day. The challenge is to stretch it to a month, then a quarter, then a half year, then a year. If you make it through your first year, you're well on your way.

If you want to get Juiced, you need some VOEMA: that's Visualize, Outcome-anticipation, Environment, Massive Action and Assess-Adjust-Adapt-Accelerate. Commit to taking these five power-steps to Spectacular Customer Service now. If you're just interested in doing them, you never will. If you are fully committed to doing them, they are already done. You're just in lag time.

1. **Visualize:** *"You can tell how many seeds are in the apple, but not how many apples are in the seed." Ken Kersey*

   What is the image that you want your Customers to have of you? After dealing with you, what do you want them to say about you to their friends and colleagues? Act the way you want your Customers to remember you. There is no such thing as an unimportant Customer or an unimportant interaction. Every time you interface with a Customer you are really preparing yourself to go further.

   See the image and step into it. Your brain cannot tell the difference between what you vividly imagine and what's really happening.

   If you use your imagination, believe your imagination and apply your imagination, you'll become all you can imagine.

   That's the difference between the Customer Service Champions and the mediocre performers. The mediocre performers do not take time out to prepare themselves for Greatness. They do not believe in "the power of the mind". And so they get caught up in the everyday problems of Customer Service and never take themselves to the next level.

Do you know how the Webster's dictionary defines Imagination? It's awesome. **Imagination:** *The action of forming mental images of what is not actually present to the senses; the power of reproducing images stored in the memory under the suggestion of associated images; the power of recombining former experiences in the creation of new images directed at a specific goal or aiding in the solution of problems; the ability to meet and resolve difficulties; resourcefulness.* So from today, use this enormous resource that may be lying unused inside your skull.

Think of yourself as a ball attached to the middle of a rope which is being pulled in two opposing directions. The one direction is where you are now. The other direction is your vision of yourself in the future. If your vision of yourself is a powerful motivational force, you will be pulled towards it. If you do not have a vision of yourself, or if it is weak and unclear, you will stay where you are forever.

Come on, visualize the kind of image your Customers are going to have of you by the end of this year. Visualize the kind of service you're going to deliver. Visualize the success you're going to enjoy. Visualize all the ways you're going to help all the people around you. Sharpen your axe. Do this as many times a day as you can. It only takes a few minutes each time. Write down your Vision for yourself, your service, your image. Just do it. It works.

Make the vision immediate. Most of us can't wait too long to be satisfied. Make a contract with your people and make it competitive. People love leadership. But it must be the kind of leadership that delivers short-term results. Very few people have the ability to keep on making sacrifices for something that may or may not happen in the long run. In fact, as John Maynard Keynes said, "In the long run, we're all dead anyway." What's more, in many big companies, the overall results are far removed from the individual business units.

So here's what we suggest: draw up a one-month mini business plan. Set your team an ambitious but achievable target that feeds into the overall vision. Consult with them on how they will achieve this target. Agree on a reward or bonus with them. And then enter into a contract with them. This is not a formal, legally binding contract. It is simply a commitment that all of you will play full out to achieve the target.

Make it competitive as well. The best players love to compete. So introduce the thrill of competition into the mix. Establish the benchmarks. Broadcast the scores. And watch the esprit de corps build.

Always have something pleasurable pending. How do you feel when you wake up on a Monday morning? How do you feel on your first day back at work in January, or after you've come back from holiday? Are you ecstatic? Or are you just a little bit blue as you think of the great time you've just had and the tough time ahead of you?

On the other hand, how do you feel on Thursday as you think of the exciting weekend you've planned? How do you feel the week before you go on holiday? What happens to your morale when you know you're going on conference to a game park tomorrow?

Here's what we believe: people always need to have something to look forward to. They cannot provide spectacular Customer Service if they are not turned on. And they cannot be turned on if they are living on a diet of endless crises and problems. Even Shakespeare said, "We are such stuff as dreams are made on." So as we write this book, thoughts of its launch in July 2000 are keeping us going. We are planning the promotion of the book while we write these words. We can see the great success of JUICED! And every time we think of it, we get even more motivated.

So what are you looking forward to? What's the dream that's sustaining you through the week? If you are a team leader, how are you incentivizing your people? It may not take much. It may just be a day trip or company picnic. It may be a motivational session delivered by a well-known speaker. It may be a night out at the movies with spouses. It may be lunch at a nice restaurant somewhere. It may be the prospect of bonuses because business is going well. The point is that it doesn't really matter what the "pleasurable something" is. What matters is that there is a "pleasurable something". Don't wait until the end of the year to have a company lunch or party. Have an event as often as possible – every week or month or quarter. And what's more, have it with Customers. Become known as the company that is closest to its Customers. Become known as the company that excels in making its Customers happy. Just like you, your Customer needs to have something to look forward to as well.

The Masterpiece Principle – Set out to create a Masterpiece and you may just succeed.

You won't believe this but we learnt this principle from our dentist. This is a truly remarkable man. Every time he completes a new filling, he steps back and exclaims loudly, "Now that's a Masterpiece! That's a work of art!" Then he smiles broadly and nods his head up and down in self-congratulation. Two things happen when he does this: firstly, as his Customers, we feel good about the filling we've just received. Isn't that amazing? Secondly, and as important, he feels good about what he's just done. He never thinks, "Oh heck, another filling!" Instead, he thinks, "Yes! Another opportunity to create a Masterpiece!!"

We suspect that our dentist consciously reminds himself of the Masterpiece Principle with every filling precisely so that he can stay motivated. He has made the decision to serve his Customers with passion, professionalism and fun. And if he can do it as a dentist, anyone can.

You know what else? If you set out to create a Masterpiece, you very often succeed. You hold yourself to a higher standard. You keep growing and stretching. What's more, you help everyone around you do the same. But if your only aspiration is to get through the day, you may not. One day you could find yourself downsized, rationalized, outsourced or vaporized. The mediocre and average performers are highly vulnerable. They are eminently dispensable. In fact, their absence could even increase the effectiveness of the organization

So what Masterpiece are you going to create today? Come on, write it down now. And make sure that you start creating it in the next 24 hours. If you wait longer than that, it could be too late. The stronger your desire to create Masterpieces, the more successful you will become. We guarantee it. In fact, right now, there's a Masterpiece inside you just waiting to get out. Give it a chance.

2. **Outcome-anticipation: Let's ask you this question:** Who are the most sought-after people in business today? We believe they're those people who have

the ability to anticipate their Customers' desired outcome even before their Customers do. If you really want to deliver Spectacular Customer Service, begin anticipating where your Customer wants to go before your Customer even asks you to go there. Nothing will impress a Customer more than your anticipation of his needs. Of course, this assumes that you've done your homework and you know what his needs and wants are.

There are so few people who are prepared to apply the Little Extra Touch. It's not a case of going the extra mile, it's a case of going the extra inch. But that Little Extra Touch will pay massive dividends. Think about your Customers right now. Think about their most desired outcome when it comes to your service. Then think about how you can surprise the Customer by anticipating what he wants and giving it to him before he asks you for it. A great example of anticipation is the Four Seasons Hotel Group, a international chain of 5-star hotels. Everyday, a Four Seasons "Review" team studies the suite Guest list. If they notice you'll be bringing children, colourful helium-filled balloons and a tray of home-made biscuits and milk will be waiting. If you're bringing your dog, there will be food bowls, doggy treats and a doggy toy – and the staff will be lined up to take little Rufus for a walk.

Planning with intent to please.

At Protea Hotels, a little acronym called SALT guides the Outcome-anticipation. Simply, Protea Hotels want to ensure that all conferences held at their venues are absolute successes. And yet more conferences fail because of lack of attention to SALT than to any other factor. SALT stands for seating, audio, lighting and temperature.

Another way Protea Hotels practises Outcome-anticipation is the speed with which they respond to Tour Operators. It can take the competitors days to respond to

Tour Operators. Protea are committed to responding within 30 minutes. The Outcome of that kind of action is that Protea Hotels get a disproportionate share of the Tour market. They are seen to be more responsive than the competition and the Tour Operators look good by being able to get back to their Customers faster.

However, it's in the planning of conferences that Outcome-anticipation really plays a massive role. Often Protea Hotels are briefed in May about a conference that will happen in December. They need to think through all the issues around that event. They need to plan the event so that it's a scintillating success, not just so that nothing goes wrong. It's called planning with intent to please. Their desired Outcome is a delighted Client and an outstanding conference. Everything is worked back from there.

Let's take another common example: dining out. When you go to a restaurant with your friends or family, you want a fabulous experience. You don't just want someone to plonk down the menu in front of you and then come back five minutes later for the order. You want someone who is going to walk you through your choices and even make ordering the food a great experience. So prepare yourself and your staff accordingly. We meet so many companies and so many people who lose the game before it's even started because they didn't practise Outcome-anticipation.

If you want a great Outcome, educate your Customers simply on how to do business with you. Otherwise, why expect them to read a manual when they can spend six months working out how to do it by themselves?

Education is preparation. Let's ask you: how many of your suppliers or vendors have educated you on how to buy from them? Less than ten percent, right? Second question: of those suppliers who have tried to educate you, how many of them made it really simple? Less than one percent, right? How many problems have you experienced because your suppliers didn't show you how to buy from them correctly or, once you have bought from them, how to use their products or services? Plenty, right? So how come 99% of companies don't take this simple step? Who knows? Maybe it's so obvious, they haven't thought of it.

Listen, whether you're selling CDs, computers or Karioke lessons, help your Customers buy from you. In a simple, enjoyable way, show them how to get the most from you. Don't expect them just to get it by themselves. We're sure you agree with us, this is really basic. Yet, hardly anyone is doing it right. It's just another reason why we believe that Spectacular Customer Service is simply about doing the basics right consistently.

Do not allow Customers to be caught by surprise. Practise the "Toothache Principle". Lessons from Federal Express.

Have you ever had toothache? How did it start? With a tiny, gentle throb, right? What did you do? Nothing, right? Did it go away by itself? Uh-uh, it got worse, right? What did you do? You just took a Panado or Aspirin, right? Did it go away by itself? Uh-uh, it got so bad you had to go to the dentist, right? So why didn't you go to the dentist right away? Why did you wait so long? Why didn't you take care of the problem before it became so painful? Fear of even more pain, right?

Like your toothache, if you don't take care of a problem while it's a baby, it's going to grow into a monster which could really hurt you. In fact, learn to identify "preproblems". These are issues which are not yet problems but which could become problems if you don't take action now. The Customer Service Champions anticipate problems or crises that may occur so that Customers can deal with them in advance rather then be forced to react to them under stress and pressure.

Here's a great example from Federal Express (FedEx) featured in Fortune Magazine 24 May 1999. At the end of 1998, the FedEx pilots threatened to strike. The Vice President for Marketing and Customer Service – David Schoenfeld's first thought was for the company's relationship with its Customers. Recent strikes at archrival UPS and Northwest Airlines had made it clear what not to do: *allow Customers to be caught by surprise.*

Shoenfeld decided that the best way to deliver the news straight up was via the company's Website. "Long before there was even the slightest hint of a concrete fear, we went out on site," Shoenfeld says. Soon a daily Pilot Negotiation Update box appeared on the first screen of fedex.com, putting updates just a click away. Telemarketers were converted to e-mail address collectors, allowing messages to be pushed out to over 30 000 Customers. Even FedEx invoices bore a line pointing Customers to the Website for news. As it turned out there was no strike, but the Website had prepared Customers for the worst.

Now, let's ask you this question: how many times have your suppliers or partners let you down because they didn't tell you about an impending problem until it was too late? More people get into trouble over their inability to warn their Customers of potential problems than almost any other issue. So from today, don't be scared to warn your Customers of a problem. Anticipate your desired Outcome – a Customer that does not want to be caught by surprise.

Ten Outcome-anticipation questions to help you prepare for Spectacular Customer Service.

The best thing about anticipating Customers' needs is that just by thinking about them, you begin to come up with solutions. We believe that the main reason why most people do not anticipate their desired Outcome is because they simply do not think about it. Even the Good Book says, "Ask and you will receive". If you ask the right questions, you'll get the right answers.

You know what else? You don't have to be years or even months ahead of the Customer in anticipating her needs. You just have to be a heartbeat ahead. But you have to do it constantly. It's not good enough being ahead of the game some of the time, you have to be ahead of the game all the time. So once you start walking down the path of Outcome-anticipation, you have to keep walking. There's no turning back. Are you up to the challenge? Of course you are, otherwise you wouldn't be over half way through the book. And congratulations, by the way, for making it this far. Only about one out of ten people who bought this book actually got this far. To reward you, we'd like to give you a free audio-cassette. All you have to do is give us feedback on the book by visiting www.mikelipkin.com or faxing us on (011) 728-6907.

To help you on your way, here are ten Outcome-anticipation questions that will open up the future for you and your Customers:

1. *What can we do to make the Customer love us forever?*
2. *How can we make it better?*
3. *What's the next big thing?*
4. *How can we take away the Customer's biggest headache?*
5. *What would really excite the Customer?*

6. *What would the Customer do and how can we do it for him?*
7. *What would really please the Customer's Customers?*
8. *How can we go where no-one has ever gone before?*
9. *How can we make it supremely memorable?*
10. *How can we help make the Customer successful?*

3. Environment – the incubator of Spectacular Customer Service. Are you receiving Juiced service from your colleagues?

You absorb the environment you work in. So what kind of environment do you work in? Is it Juiced? Is it energized? Is it supportive? Is it conducive to Spectacular Customer Service? In fact, here's a quick Customer Service test: *what kind of service are you receiving from your colleagues?* How responsive are the other business units or departments to you? We can promise you this: if you deliver Spectacular Service to your colleagues and they reciprocate, you will deliver Spectacular Service to your Customers. However, if the service between colleagues is mediocre, then the service to Customers will be exactly the same.

A Juiced environment is the incubator of Spectacular Customer Service. And like an incubator, it has to be carefully designed, prepared and monitored. A Juiced environment may be the most important overall element in the delivery of Spectacular Service. Is yours? How much investment have you made in growing a Juiced environment? Or have you just let the environment evolve by itself? Or, even if you're a frontline service person, what are you doing to Juice up your environment?

Do this exercise: when you visit Customers, suppliers, stores and restaurants, look around you, absorb their environments, ask yourself whether they're Juiced or not, then ask yourself why you think that. We believe that you'll find the Juiced environments are populated by people who are Juiced. You'll find that they enjoy each other. You'll find that they move quickly but purposefully around their workplace. You'll see people smiling and you'll hear the sound of laughter. There will be a sense of cohesion and integration. People will be having quick chats in the corridors. There will be touches of colour around the place. And, we're willing to bet you, people will greet you and ask you whether you've been attended to. You'll feel an immediate sense of attraction to the company. You'll even feel at home.

On the other hand, visit the Juiceless companies and you'll feel the stress as you walk through the door. You'll see people who are pressurized, scared, pessimistic and anxious. You'll hear people blaming and badmouthing their own companies. You'll feel a little uncomfortable even though you don't work there. Even the physical nature of the company's premises will lack warmth and charm. We're also willing to bet that you'll find cartoons and notes on the wall that make fun of productivity, Customers and service.

So how do you create a Juiced environment? Well, it begins with making sure the people in your company use a Juiced vocabulary.

At Protea Hotels, it's a serious offence to smile at the Guest and then go into the back office and badmouth or mock him. Respect for the Guest is paramount. It must run through the entire organization. It just takes one person with a bad attitude to begin destroying respect for the Guest. Too many companies tolerate insulting language about the Customer behind the Customer's back. This is a cancer that will kill the company. There is no way that you'll be able to hide your contempt for the Customer over time. If people within the company talk badly about the Customer, it will trickle back to the frontline. The Customer will eventually feel it. And when that happens, you're dead. What's more, the Customer will tell at least 100 people about his bad experience with you. Talking badly about others is a boomerang that will come back and bruise you badly.

So let's ask you: do you ever talk badly about your Customers? Do you ever moan and complain about them to your colleagues after a meeting or a phone call? Remember, words are real. Elephants have got nothing on human beings. Human beings never forget. Sticks and stones can break your bones, but words will screw up your life forever. We can handle the physical hurts but the emotional scars never go away.

This point is especially important in a culturally diverse country such as South Africa. Right now, South Africans are still extremely sensitive to slights and slurs. We all need to be extremely careful to show not just our respect for each other, but our affection.

And by the way, this principle applies to the way you speak to your kids as well. It breaks our hearts when we hear parents saying to their children: don't be so stupid; stop being such a nuisance; are you deaf; how many times do I have to tell you. . . . Remember, with every word and every action, you are creating the person your child is becoming. And most of the time, if you really think about it, our children bear the brunt of our stress and tension. We become angry with them not because of what they've done, but because of the way we feel.

Quick, what goes through your mind when you hear the word, "Juiced!"? Your thoughts and words are really units of human energy that either move you towards happiness or

away from it. Vocabulary is vital so go on a mental diet.

Come on, say it aloud, "JUICED!" What do you think about? Oranges, cold, sweet, bright, enjoyable, tasty, fresh, refreshing, nutritious, thirst-quenching, healthy, excited, youthful, energetic, pumped, invigorated, motivated, turned-on, love, active, alive, passionate, fun, movement, playfulness, fit, fully committed, dynamic, smiling and laughing.

We spent many hours thinking up a title for this book that would express its spirit. In the middle of one brainstorming session, we hit on the word "Juiced!" because it just said what we're all about. It expressed our joy and love for what we're doing and how that makes us feel. In fact, every time we even say the word, "Juiced!" we actually become Juiced.

It's true. You become the thoughts you have and the words you use. Your thoughts and words are really units of human energy that either move you towards happiness or away from it.

To prove our point, please read the following words aloud: depressed, sad, angry, disappointed, cross, annoyed, tense, down, demoralized, betrayed, idiot, fool, enemy, crisis, mistake, pain, failure, hate, fight, argument, conflict, heart attack. How are you feeling right now? Pretty unJuiced, right?

Now read these words aloud: Oranges, cold, sweet, bright, enjoyable, tasty, fresh, refreshing, nutritious, thirst-quenching, healthy, excited, youthful, energetic, pumped, invigorated, motivated, turned-on, love, active, alive, passionate, fun, movement, playfulness, fit, fully committed, dynamic, smiling and laughing. How do you feel now? Pretty darn Juiced, right?

You are the sovereign ruler of everything that goes on between your ears. Govern yourself well.

So what are the words that you use every day? Are you using Juiced language or words of defeat? Do this exercise with us: look at your watch. For the next 30 seconds, please sit still and watch the second hand move. Do it now. Do not read on until you've done this exercise.

Welcome back. What did you hear while you watched your watch? Yes, you probably heard some sounds outside. But what did you hear inside your head? In other words, what thoughts were you listening to? Did you say to yourself, "This is a dumb exercise!", or did you ask yourself why you were being asked to do it? Or did your mind just wander?

What's our point? We are all continually thinking. And what is thinking but talking to ourselves? Did you know that you think at the rate of 800 words a minute, but you speak at the rate of about 200 words a minute. That means while someone else is speaking to you, you are speaking to yourself four times as much. And the words you're using determine your moods, your attitude, your happiness and, ultimately, your success or failure.

People and companies who sustain a high level of success have the ability to talk to themselves and to others in a consistently empowering way. Even when they feel the need to use disempowering language, they discipline themselves not to vent their negative emotions on the people around them. Do you?

Many of us have got into the habit of speaking negatively. We've become used to moaning and groaning. And we do it without even being aware of it. Well, from today, make a conscious decision to use Juiced language. It's probably the only thing in your life that you can control. You are 100% in charge of your mental territory. You are the sovereign ruler of everything that goes on between your ears. Govern yourself well. And help all around you to do the same. The best companies are filled with people who walk the turned-on talk. They contribute to the environment and the environment constantly recharges them. It's a continual cycle, as natural as the rain that falls from the sky.

Lessons from Mickey Mouse, Donald Duck and Pluto.

It's not surprising that Customers are automatically attracted to Juiced companies. They buy your optimism, warmth, hope and energy as much as the product or service that you sell. Walt Disney is possibly the most vivid illustration in the world of this truth. Besides being one of the world's most successful companies, it is widely acknowledged as the world champion in Customer Service. Did you know that Disney has its own vocabulary? Here is a sample of it. At Disney:

You don't do a job, you play a role
You don't put on a uniform, you wear a costume
You're not an employee, you're a castmember
You don't do business with Customers, you serve Guests
Your mission is to create happiness for Guests
When you're in front of a Guest, "you're on stage"
When you're preparing to go in front of a Guest, "you're backstage"
When you do well, you've put on a "Good Show"
When you mess up, you've put on a "Bad show"

What is the vocabulary of your company? If you don't have one, begin building a Juiced vocabulary today.

Immerse your staff in the traditions of your company. Give them a Golden Lemon.

If we were to ask your frontline people about the traditions or heritage of your company, what would they tell us? Would they struggle to describe what your company's all about? Do they have a clear understanding of where the company's come from and where it's going?

At Protea Hotels, the right talent is hired. Then people are trained in the traditions of the company. Every employee who is hired is exposed to a day and a half orientation programme – Traditions: the traditions of how things are done at Protea Hotels. This is delivered in a classroom. Delegates are immersed in the "Protea Hotel's Way". Specifically, they are taught the service ethos of Protea. The orientation programme is then followed up by an ongoing on-the-job training programme.

Part of the orientation programme is a zany video featuring Arthur and other top management doing a rock 'n roll number called: "Smiling on the Ceiling." In this video, staff are given the Ten Golden Keys to service. It is funny and up front, new employees are taught not to put people on pedestals. Staff call Arthur by his first name. They are encouraged to be relaxed in his presence. And they are encouraged to tell top management when they think top management is screwing up.

You know what else? Protea Hotels actually celebrates those people who've made the biggest screw-ups in the company. Seriously, they have a prize called the Golden Lemon Award that is given to the individual who made the most monumental mistake of the year. Invariably, this award is won by a member of top management who collects his trophy at a big function specifically called to mark the occasion. In Academy Award style, he is called up to make a speech as he walks off with his "Golden

Lemon". The thinking behind the award is to de-stigmatize mistakes and encourage people to act out of passion, purpose and care for the Customer, not out of fear of being wrong. What are you doing in your company to build a Juiced Culture and help people deal with their fear of change and failure?

At Research Surveys, there are no "backroom people". Everyone is in Customer Service. Everyone matters.

Henry Barenblatt, CEO of Research Surveys – South Africa's largest consumer research company, tells this story that we loved because it illustrates the power of a Juiced environment to Juice people to deliver Spectacular Customer Service: The South African Breweries (SAB) is Research Survey's biggest Customer. At 20h00 one evening, Research Surveys received a call from a senior executive at SAB. He was trying to get hold of an account executive who had already left. SAB had an issue that they wanted to resolve immediately.

The person who answered the phone was Jamiela, a computer operator. Jamiela asked the SAB executive if she could help him and then proceeded to handle all his queries with knowledge and confidence. The SAB executive was mightily impressed because he knew that he was talking to a computer operator. Henry heard about this occurrence the next day from the SAB executive who called him specifically to compliment Jamiela. Research Surveys rewarded Jamiela by flying her up to Johannesburg to introduce her personally to SAB.

Why did Jamiela do what she did? Well, according to Henry she felt empowered to take charge of the situation. She had come up through the ranks. She took responsibility. She had been given numerous opportunities to meet and interact with Customers. She had been involved in the SAB project. The ethos of Research Surveys also encourages people to be accountable and take action. Research Surveys, according to Barenblatt, does not have "backroom people". Everyone is in Customer Service. Everyone knows what their end-goal is: Absolutely pleasing the Customer. That's why Customers are encouraged to come into their offices and talk about their products and services to staff.

Research Surveys is also a member of the Adcorp Group, a listed company on the Johannesburg Stock Exchange. Every year, the Chairman of the group – Van Zyl Slabbert, talks about the company's performance to every single member of staff, so that everyone knows what Adcorp is all about and the challenges it faces. There is a ceremonial value in this act. It symbolizes that, whether you're the mailman or the chairman, everyone matters.

Never underestimate the power of ceremony and symbolism to boost staff morale and commitment.

The Diamond Concept: how to polish each other's skills so that they shine brightly for the Customer.

One of the questions asked of Protea Hotels is why there appears to be so little envy or discord throughout the organization. The answer is the Diamond Concept. Here's how it works: if someone comes up with an idea, it's like they've mined the diamond. However, the idea is still imperfect. But there's no way that you can throw a diamond away. Instead, it's passed around and as it's passed around, more people polish and add facets to it. At the end of the process, the company has a jewel because each person has added their insight to it.

The Diamond Concept works so well because it's all about finding complementary relationships with your team members. We even applied it in the creation of this book. Arthur's skill is describing and depicting issues in such a way that people "get it" immediately. Mike's skill is taking out the core principle of an experience and sharing it with others. The Diamond Concept allowed us to polish each other's talents and produce a jewel.

In many companies, however, we encounter the Not-Invented-Here syndrome. That is when people actively sabotage or discard ideas because they didn't originate from them or from their departments. The result is friction, not friendship between departments. Relationships break down and so does Customer Service.

"I want to thank God for giving me the talent and the forwards for giving me the ball." Jannie de Beer. **Spectacular Customer Service is a team sport.**

If you are a South African and you love Rugby, then South Africa's victory over England in the quarter-final of the 1999 Rugby World Cup must have been a highlight for you – especially Jannie de Beer's world-record-breaking five drop-kicks.

We believe that Jannie's quote, as featured above, is one of the all-time greats because it expresses perfectly the factors that go into Spectacular Customer Service: gratitude, talent, teamwork, co-ordination, interplay between team-members, humility, belief in a Higher Power, love-of-the-game, protection, preparation, a gameplan, practise and idealism. Are these the qualities that characterize your working environment? Because if they are absent, there is no way you can captivate the Customer with Spectacular Service. Naysayers, cynics, pessimists and loners can never sustain a winning season.

So far, we've spoken about the environment in your company and in your cranium. But it's the external environment that impacts the Customer. Use it or lose it. Do you have "Insider Status"?

How clued up are you on what's happening in your market? How clued up are you on what's happening in your country? How clued up are you on what's happening on your continent? How clued up are you about what's happening in the world? Your answers to all these questions will determine your ability to truly deliver Spectacular Customer Service.

The Customer Service Champions are valuable resources to their Customers. They help their Customers in ways that go beyond the actual service or product they sell to them. For example, when a company calls Mike to deliver a workshop, Mike shares his knowledge of global trends in the Customer's business based on working in 13 countries, speaking to over 200 000 people, reading a new book every ten days, browsing relevant websites and actually writing books of this nature. Mike will help design the entire conference and suggest ways of extending the output of the conference into the ongoing operation of the organisation.

Our message here is: understand the external environment so that you can use it to get closer to your Customers. Nothing will turn on a Customer more than your understanding of their context and challenges. And nothing will turn off a Customer faster than your ignorance.

How close are you really to your Customer? Do you pass the "Insider Status" test? Insider Status means that you've been accepted as part of the Customer's inner circle. You have crossed the line from supplier to partner.

You find your Customer sharing inside knowledge with you on what's going on within his company. He even tells you what your competition is doing. And, most importantly, he asks you for advice on issues that are not even directly related to the service you're providing him. When you've achieved Insider Status, you're Golden.

4. Massive Action: words are one thing, actions are another. Beware of SOROV and don't wobble. It just takes 1% a week.

You know what? As far as Customer Service leadership is concerned, there is no one blueprint. Some leaders lead from the front. Others quietly coach from the sidelines. Others constantly cheerlead the people around them in a high energy style. Still others walk behind their people so that their people can shine. The style is not what's important. What is important is that Customer Service Leaders are their vocabulary-in-motion. They set the tempo of the organisation. They operate out of integrity. They do not allow themselves the luxury of slacking off. They are continually taking the next step up and inspiring their people to do the same.

Why have we used the words "Massive Action" here? Because once you know your vision and desired outcome, you must take Massive Action to make it happen. Not adequate action, not sufficient action but Massive Action. This is where the rubber meets the road. Spectacular Customer Service all hinges on execution.

We meet so many people who know what to do but they don't do what they know. There is a big knowing-doing gap that prevents the delivery of Spectacular Customer Service. They SOROV do it. SOROV is not a Russian philosopher. It's a term coined by Professor Ian Bellis. It means that when you ask people whether they did the job well, their response is "SOROV". SOROV is an attitude that says 60-70% exertion will suffice. SOROV is when your colleagues get by on as little as possible firstly, because they may not be motivated to give more and secondly, because they may not know how to give more.

At Protea Hotels, the primary mechanism to ensure that staff never SOROV, or sort of, do anything is the "OEM – optimal experience map". The OEM documents the kind of experience that Guests should have. Then it provides the guidelines that need to be followed. For example, the ideally made-up room is photographed so that staff know exactly how it's supposed to look when they are finished with it. If you want your people to perform, make sure they know exactly what your expectations are and how they can get there. If the expectations are not clear, everything else ends up in a mess.

Remember these thirteen Massive Action words:

> *If you sit, just sit. If you stand, just stand. But don't wobble.*

If you're going to serve someone, then serve him. If you're not going to serve him, then don't. But don't SOROV serve him. Whatever you do, do it with gusto and vigour.

And the good news is that you don't need to take a quantum leap from here to there. All you need to do is to enhance your performance by 1% a week. Then each time you improve by another 1%, you are improving off a higher base and the magic of compound interest begins working for you. Steady Susan in week one can become Spectacular-Service Susie by week 52. Did you know that if you improve just 1% a week, you'll improve by 67% a year thanks to compound interest. So begin now because, if not now, when?

Get Congruent – the ultimate secret of highly successful Customer Service providers.

Quick, when you meet people for the first time, how do you immediately decide whether or not you want to deal with them? Isn't it the way they stand, talk and look at you? Isn't it their boldness, confidence, friendliness and openness? Isn't it the fact that their words seem to match their actions? You feel as though they are genuine and authentic. In other words, you feel as though you can trust them.

You are congruent when your words, your voice, your body language and your actions all reinforce each other. You are not congruent when what you are saying and what you are feeling are not unified. Saying one thing while you're feeling another is the quickest way to lose Customers. You know why? Because all of us have built in "lie detectors". We can tell when someone is not being genuine. We see it all the time. How many times has someone said, "Have a nice day" or "Welcome" or "Come back soon" or "How are you?" without really caring? Doesn't it drive you nuts?

Well, you know what? 90% of people are exactly like that. They don't operate in a congruent fashion. You know why? Because they're not thinking of you while they're speaking to you. They are not truly happy to be serving you. They'd rather be somewhere else and their mind probably is. So you are getting a very small part of them – and not the most pleasing part either. What about you? How much of yourself are you giving the people around you?

Remember, people buy for emotional reasons. To make an emotional decision, like trusting you, they need to feel certain that what you're saying is true. If you aren't congruent, you will send out an aura of indecision and weakness. So your personal congruency is your ability to project absolute certainty in voice, word and body that whatever you are saying is true. Start practising this today and enjoy the instant benefits. Let us know the results by visiting www.mikelipkin.com or by faxing us on (011) 728-6907 and leaving us a message

Massive action also means investing in yourself. Learning is power. Just like computer programmes, you need to upgrade your mental software every week, every month or, at least, every year. If you want to deliver Spectacular Customer Service, learn how to cook or weave baskets. Experience is only valuable when you stay new.

Let's ask you: what have you done to upgrade yourself in terms of ongoing education over the past week? Over the past month? Over the past year? What have you done to make yourself more valuable in the marketplace? What new skills have you acquired over the past twelve months? What skills have you sharpened recently? How have you Juiced your mind?

It doesn't matter whether you've attended a seminar, read a book, listened to a CD or taken on a new responsibility that requires new and different skills. The point is to ensure that your brain is constantly being stretched. Did you know that your brain expands according to the challenges you give it? Seriously, every time you ask your brain to think of something new, it grows new connections that utilize parts that were not used before. If you want to stay young in your head, stay a student. An unchallenged mind is a dying mind. A mind that is not growing is a mind that is being wasted. And a human mind is a terrible thing to waste.

You know what else? It doesn't even matter what

you're learning – whether it's calculus, cooking or basket weaving. What matters is that you're keeping your mind agile. We promise you that you will not be able to handle the accelerating speed of change if your mind isn't as agile as an acrobat. Experience alone is no guarantee of success. In fact, in the future, experience may even be a liability. Just look at the amount of long-serving employees who are being rationalized out of their companies. Experience is only valuable when you stay new and stimulated. If you allow yourself to become stale and bored, the end is near. Bored people deliver atrocious service because they don't give a darn and they've got no Juice. We'll tell you this, though: you're a person who believes in self-development. If you weren't, you wouldn't be reading these pages. Your mission now must be to help us motivate others to go out there and learn. Copy this page if you like and give to someone you know. You have our permission. Go make a difference and you'll grow in the process.

One of the reasons we've written this book is simply to stretch ourselves. It's another mountain that we've climbed. Our muscles hurt like heck but they're a lot stronger now than they were before we started this journey. What's more, it was a huge amount of fun. Does it seem like we're Juiced? Absolutely!

And, by the way, we know that you're taking care of your body. We hope that you're working out, watching your diet, avoiding smoking and excessive drinking. If you want to deliver Spectacular Customer Service, you need to radiate vitality and health. People are attracted to people who are fit and healthy. Yet, did you know that less than 5% of all South Africans actually work out? Please, become one of them.

Become a Go-Giver not a Go-Getter. Charity is good business.

"Everything we own is on loan and service is the interest we pay on our debt." Mahatma Gandhi

The real Customer Service champions are always giving. They are not only motivated by direct remuneration for services rendered. In fact, they get more Juice out of giving just for its own sake. We promise you that if you see your community as your Customers and you serve them the way the way you serve your best Customers, you will be paid back hundredfold. You know how? Not just in spiritual compensation but in the goodwill that your charity generates. People like to do business with people who help others. Being a good citizen pays. If you develop a reputation for being a generous and caring person, business will flood to you.

We know. Both of us invest big chunks of our time and money in serving the community. Yes, we do it because we love to do it. But we also do it because we have no choice. Service is how we pay our mortgages to the great account keeper in the sky. It's how we show our gratitude. And we'll say this to you right now: if you are not prepared to give some of your time to helping people less fortunate than you, you are an oxygen thief. Every single member of the community who is physically able to give must give. If you don't, it will all be taken away. Seriously, both of us speak to hundreds of people who lament their financial or business losses. We know that for almost all of them, it was because they didn't use their resources to help others.

So from this moment on, see acts of charity as spiritual insurance. We're sure you know as well as we do, every time you make a deposit into your spiritual insurance account, you feel extraordinary. Come on, make a deposit today. Do it right now. And then contact us on www.mikelipkin.com or fax us on (011) 728-6907 and tell us what you did.

The Rotary Club has a guiding principle that we believe should be everyone's beacon. It's simply: *Service Above Self.* If you serve something greater than yourself, you become greater. If you are only concerned about yourself, you become a dwarf. You know what else? The more you give, the more you feel you can give. You develop what Stephen Covey calls an Abundance Mentality. You feel as though you have plenty and so you attract plenty to you. On the other hand, if you don't give because you feel you have nothing to give or you just can't be bothered, you'll develop a Scarcity Mentality and you'll have less and less.

Build up a reservoir of goodwill before you need it. Give more than others think is wise and you will have the last laugh.

Ultimately, Spectacular Customer Service is all about building up a reservoir of goodwill with Customers. The greater the reservoir of goodwill, the greater your Customers' commitment to you. So seize every opportunity you can to build goodwill. Seize the big opportunities and seize the small ones. Because we promise you that there will come a time when you will make a mistake with this Customer. If you don't have a reservoir of Goodwill, you're dead. If you do, you may just get a second chance and even a third.

So for example, in the hotel business, one of the worst things you can do is to upgrade a Guest to a better room or a suite and not tell them why they're being upgraded. Why? Because the real reason may be that you're overbooked on standard rooms and the suite is the only space available. But if you tell the Guest that, they're not going to feel special. Instead, you need to let the Guest know how lucky she is. You need to really dramatize the benefits of the suite and all its facilities. If this Guest is a frequent visitor, then you need to position this upgrade as a reward for her loyalty. In that way, you will make emotional capital out of the situation that will pay a high return over time. The same principle applies to any other industry.

To conclude this point, let's ask you another question: how do you feel about people who only call you when they need something from you? A little annoyed or irritated, right? Now let's ask you: how often do you only call people when you need something from them? What's the lesson here? Keep doing favours for people. We promise you that at some stage, you're going to draw on them. The secret is to do the favour when you can afford to – not when you're forced to.

Invoke the Law of Reciprocation: one of the most powerful tools in Customer Service you can use. It's amazing what R3.74 can still buy you. Start your own informal loyalty programme.

From the earliest age, we are conditioned to believe that if someone gives something to us, we need to give something back. Or if someone does us a favour, we need to return it. Here's an example: if someone says something nice to you, don't you usually say something nice back? Or if someone invites you for dinner, don't you feel obliged to return the invitation? Or if someone thanks you in a really warm, genuine way, don't you say, "It's a pleasure"? That's why it's very difficult not to like someone who likes us. The truth is that people will do more for others out of the pressure of obligation than for almost any other reason.

When someone does something for us, we begin to experience an unconscious – and sometimes conscious, pressure to reciprocate. It is a programmed pattern installed in most of us. So any time you can give something to a Customer that they don't expect, do it. You've just invested in a massive future payback. In all but the rarest cases, the other person will come through for you when you need him most.

Recently Mike was asked by a Customer to give a talk to a group of students in Cape Town and Johannesburg. Although money wasn't discussed, there was an unspoken agreement that these sessions were to be delivered free. Four months later, Mike staged a series of public seminars across the country. He asked this Customer to send a few delegates. Well, guess how many the Customer sent? 150. This Customer almost single-handedly made the seminars a financial success.

In May 2000, while this book was being written, Mike went one night to the Spar in Sea Point, Cape Town, to buy some groceries. His bill came to R103.74. He only had R100 on him so he was about to return a tin of tuna for R5 when the manager told him he could pay the R3.74 the next time he came into the store. This small act of generosity made Mike return there three more times during the next week and, of course, feature the story in this book. It's amazing what R3.74 can still buy you. What small but meaningful things can you do to invoke the Law of Reciprocation with your Customers? Start your own informal loyalty programme. Continually ask yourself the following Spectacular Customer Service question and the answers will come to you:

What can I do for my Customers that they don't expect and that's not going to cost me a lot of money but which will have a huge emotional Impact on them?

We'd like to hear from you how you're Juicing Customers through your small acts of reciprocation. Fax us on (011) 728-6907 or visit **www.mikelipkin.com**

5. Assess, Adjust, Adapt, Accelerate. Your products and services are not important. Your Customer's opinions of you are. In the Truth Economy, there's nowhere to hide. When in doubt, accelerate.

"Thanks to the Web, we now live in the Truth Economy," says Web strategist David Siegel, "People are talking to one another all the time. They're telling one another the truth about whether a certain hotel in Bangkok is as good as its ads say it is, or whether the food on one cruise line is as good as the food on a different line. The Web gives Customers what they've always wanted: a chance to express themselves, to get honest answers to their questions, and to share their interests and passions with other Customers. And it requires every company to behave differently – to let information flow freely, to participate in genuine conversations with Customers." (Fast Company April 2000)

Earlier in this book, we discussed the vital importance of feedback. The issue here is how quickly you assess the impact of the feedback, adjust your strategy, adapt to the new realities and accelerate your progress. We meet so many people who are too attached to what they're selling or doing. They get highly emotional when their ideas are criticized or rejected by Customers. Then they have difficulty adjusting and adapting to a new strategy. Well, you absolutely cannot afford to take anything personally. It's not you who is being rejected anyway. It's your idea. It's the thought or the action.

This book is a response to the re-assessment by Mike of the opinions he was receiving from his Customers. They told him: Motivation is fine and good, but we need to know how to channel all that energy into the service we provide our Customers. Mike then turned to Arthur, who is renowned for his Customer Service, to co-author this book. Juiced! is therefore a direct result of assessing, adapting and adjusting to Customers' opinions.

When in doubt, accelerate. In a web-connected world, you don't have the luxury of prolonged deliberation. The fast eat the slow. Customers are becoming incredibly demanding. They may forgive you for a bug or two in your product or service. But they won't forgive you for slowing them down. Think about yourself: what is your attitude towards suppliers or associates who keep you waiting while you have a million things to do. How do you feel about them? Exactly. So, if you do it to your Customers, they'll punish you by leaving you.

As a human being, your real competitor is a Website. It's fast, it's colourful, it's extremely knowledgeable, it's interesting, it never sleeps and it gives you exactly what you want. So how do you compete?

Recently, Mike was asked to deliver a presentation in Nairobi, Kenya. He received the e-mail at 21h15. He needed to get back to the Customer immediately. However, he also needed to know flight times because his fee was dependent the number of days spent in Kenya. The travel agency, of course, was closed so Mike clicked onto South African Airways' Website (www.saa.co.za). He told it exactly when he wanted to leave and return. He received all the information instantly. He responded to his Customer within 20 minutes of receiving the original e-mail. Compare this response to the struggle of trying to get hold of a knowledgeable, motivated SAA representative at that time. No contest. Sometimes it is really far more pleasurable to deal with the Net than a human.

So, if you're managing the Customer Service strategy of your company, make sure your Website is outstanding. Make a big investment. But make sure you know what the Customer really wants. The SAA Website, for example, didn't allow Mike to book and pay for his trip there and then.

On the other hand, if you're in the business of interacting with Customers, make sure you've got something that no Website can match – an approach that is uniquely adjusted and adapted to the Customer; a voice that radiates warmth and pleasure; an energy that motivates and inspires; an intimacy that reassures and relaxes; an eagerness to serve that enchants and captivates; and, of course, an efficiency that at least comes close to any Website.

How well are you doing on the 4 A's?

Both of us obviously deal with many suppliers and business partners every day. What we want are people who keep pace with our frenzied schedules. We have so many projects under construction that preparation and execution are almost simultaneous in many instances. That's why we've produced this book through a small printing operation called Supreme Printers. They have produced two previous books for Touch The Sky, our publishers, and their turnaround time was truly spectacular. Above all else, it was their ability to assess our request, adjust their approach, adapt to the new challenge and accelerate their delivery time that won them this sought-after contract.

How well are you doing on the 4 A's? How often are you assessing and adjusting your strategy? How effectively have you adapted to the new South African

Customer? In a shootout with the competition, who is always quickest on the draw? If you're a bit shaky on any of these questions, do some preparation now for the future. You see, you only have to be a nanosecond ahead of the competition to win big time. And the converse, unfortunately, also applies.

The Gillis-Lipkin Formula for Spectacular Customer Service Factor Four: Marketing

"Last night, we lost R2.1million in unsold rooms and food. It's called lost opportunities. And the bad news is that we're going to do it again tonight. How are you doing?" Arthur Gillis. **Welcome to Bednight Marketing: the difference between profitability and panic.**

We've explored the power of Desire, Empathy and Preparation in the design and delivery of Spectacular Customer Service. But if you don't attract Customers to you in the first place, you won't even get a chance to demonstrate how awesome you and your organization are.

Let's ask you, how much unsold downtime did you have today? How much are you going to have tomorrow? How does that make you feel? How would you like to ensure that your unsold downtime is minimized? Read on.

Both of us sell time-specific services. That means if we don't sell our services by a specific time, we'll never sell them. There is nothing as lost as last night's empty hotel room. And if you are the Managing Director of a group of over 100 hotels, there is nothing as painful as high fixed costs that are not being covered. It's business that will never come the way of Protea Hotels again. It hurts. And it's the reason why Protea Hotels are always trying to increase the speed, urgency, creativity and flexibility with which they sell rooms.

So how come Protea Hotels lost R2.1million last night in

unsold rooms? First of all, it's got nothing to do with the environment or the competition. Protea burnt those excuses a long time ago. It's got everything to do with the fact that Protea didn't attract enough Guests through Spectacular Marketing. Yes, it's easy to talk the good game. But even we struggle to always put these principles into practise. That's life. The struggle is what gives life its Juice.

Welcome to Bednight Marketing: the difference between profitability and panic. Bednight Marketing is simply the ability to attract Customers to you in the face of intense competition under extreme conditions. It is guided by a simple philosophy:

> *Sell your service profitably by doing whatever it takes to give the Customer what she wants, when she wants it, at the price she wants it, in a way that she will never forget.*

It's all about profitable standards: price drives service, service doesn't drive price. And it's the Customer who determines the price. But here's the silver bullet: It's as easy to exceed your Customer's expectations at a budget price as it is at a luxury price, if not easier.

What's a "profitable standard"? It's all the Customer Service and facilities that Protea Hotels can offer Guests while still making a profit. Of course, "profitable standards" change from Guest to Guest, hotel to hotel and season to season. Price drives service, service doesn't drive price. And it's the Guest who determines the price. For example, if you can only afford R400 a night on a room, that's all you're going to spend. Protea Hotels then have to give you as much service as they can for that price. If they give you more service than they can afford, they won't maintain a profitable standard and they'll go out of business.

People have certain expectations about what they're going to receive for their money. Obviously they know they'll get less service for R400 than they will for R800. But here's the silver bullet: It's as easy to exceed your Customer's expectations at a budget price as it is at a luxury price, if not easier. You know why? Because at R800, the expectations are extremely high. At R400, they're not. A smile or a little extra touch of any nature will make a huge difference.

Protea Hotels, like many businesses, live in an environment of high fixed costs. Their operational costs vary by less than 10% from season to season. The incremental cost of a bednight may be less than R50. So if Protea's normal rate is R400 and they are offered R60 for a room, should they take it? The answer according to Protea is a qualified "yes." It must not create discord among existing Guests. It must not move Guests down the scale so they pay less than they would have paid previously. It must be part of a package or scheme that maintains the integrity of what all Protea Guests are offered.

For example, like many businesses today, Protea Hotels often offer their facilities on auction. After all, as they say in the real estate business, a property is only worth what a buyer is willing to pay. The all-powerful lesson here is: increasingly, we're living in an oversupply situation. It is truly the Age of The Customer. She has massive choices. To make sure she chooses you, give her what she wants, when she wants it at the price she wants it. And keep your overheads low. Travel light. You can't perform somersaults if you're overweight.

The Three Legs of Bednight Marketing: Firstly, know your three kinds of Customers: Users, Decision Makers and Influencers.

"The Customer may always be right but not every Customer may be right for you." *David Siegel*

Tell us, how well do you know the people who use your product or service? Do you know them so well that you could describe them in detail to us now? And tell us, do the people who use you make the decision to use you or is the decision made by a different person? If he is different, how well do you know the decision maker? And tell us, do you know who influences the decision maker? If yes, are you influencing the Influencers? Because if you aren't, your competitor is.

If you lead people who serve Customers, we hope you've coached them on these three vital groups of stakeholders to your business. Because if you haven't, you and your people are flying blind. And if you fly blind, you tend to crash into mountains. By the way, we hope that you, as the leader, know about your Users, Decision Makers and Influencers.

If you are a front-line person and no-one has given you this information, seize the initiative and go out and get it. Find a way or make a way. Knowledge isn't just power, it's speed – especially when you know your Customers so well you can anticipate their needs, desires and responses.

We know what kind of person you are: you are committed to personal growth. You have staying power. You are successful and you're on your way to being even more successful. You are young at heart and you care for the people around you. You're a role model for others but you believe you have so much more potential to fulfil. You're a leader – whether or not you are currently managing people. And, if you're not, you soon will be. You're a professional. You operate with integrity and you're an optimist.

You may or may not have made the decision to buy this book yourself. In fact, only 50% of our readers made the decision themselves. The other 50% are reading it because it was bought for them by their companies. The Decision Makers are similar to the readers of this book, except that they're a little older. They're already where the rest of the readers want to be. And they've got there by practising a lot of the principles of this book. They come from all racial and cultural groups. They've overcome many obstacles on their way to the top. They have an unstoppable spirit. They have a sense of humour and their people love working with them.

Regarding *Juiced!*, the Influencers of the Readers and Decision Makers are the media, associates who have already read the book and other well-known and respected figures.

So, to help you really understand your three kinds of Customers, here are some aspects of them that you should explore:

- *Customer name and company*
- *Education*
- *Family*
- *Previous employment*
- *Career objectives*
- *Priorities*
- *Lifestyle*
- *Expectations of you: needs*
- *Buying process*
- *Budget*
- *Role models*
- *Competitors from whom they buy*

And remember, when it comes to finding out about your Customers, there is no greater source of information than the Web. As two marketers who have to continually get information on our Customers, we surf the Web continuously. In fact, a lot of the information you're reading in this book was sourced or inspired through free online information.

The Second Leg of Bednight Marketing: Know your USP – your Unique Selling Proposition. To put it simply: what vital benefit can you give the Customer that no-one else can? Your resources + your personality x your imagination = USP.

In times of chaos and change, he who hesitates with his Customers is not lost. He's buried. However, in times of chaos and change, he who knows exactly how to give his Customers what they need in a way that no-one else can, will be rich, famous and fulfilled.

Increasingly, we're living in a time when everything seems more and more the same. The Chicago Tribune, April 9 2000, ran an article titled, *"The end of originality. In a digital age, imitation rules."* The article went on to state that advances in technology enable virtually anything to be reproduced quickly and cheaply – including animals and maybe soon, humans. We are living, the article states, in the *"Culture of the Copy"*.

So, under these circumstances, how do you set yourself apart by offering a vital benefit that no-one else can? Our response: in South Africa, the market is still wide open. By blending your resources with your personality and using your imagination – anything is possible. Even better, this is just so simple. And by the way, this principle works as well for you as an individual as it does for a company. Try the following exercise for both yourself and your company:

To help you, we have completed this exercise for this book – *Juiced!* which is a product just like any other:

Identify Juiced!'s most valuable resources:

Hospitality, motivational and publishing experience; vibrant country; sufficient funds; sense of humour; outstanding suppliers; responsive Customers; marketing expertise and knowledge; international exposure; our ability to work at high speed and to work hard; stamina; massive doses of desire and empathy. Now you do yours.

Describe Juiced!'s personality: Bold, friendly, funny, outgoing, a little crazy, caring, reassuring, energizing, intense, confident and interdependent. Now you do yours.

Multiply Juiced!'s resources and personality by Gillis-Lipkin's imagination: What if we create South Africa's easiest-to-read, simplest, most valuable book on Customer Service ever? How about creating a book on Customer Service that is actually fun to read? What would happen if we use the hospitality model and the motivational model to turn on South Africans to Spectacular Customer Service? How can we create a book that will make a massive difference to the nation? What if the book is just the first element in a whole Spectacular Customer Service Movement? What's next? What if we can Juice enough South Africans so that South Africa becomes a world leader in Customer Service? Is it possible to help South Africans believe in themselves and in their fellow South Africans? How can we help people succeed by serving others? Can we produce a book in record-breaking time? What if we can create the first book ever that combined head and heart to help frontline people really understand what Spectacular Customer Service is all about? Now you do yours. Red light: this step takes time. It takes some brainstorming and it needs someone who can step back and facilitate the process.

Juiced!'s Unique Selling Proposition: Juiced! is the first and only book that will excite and empower all South Africans, from CEO to Cashier, to succeed through Spectacular Customer Service. Now you do yours. Red light: this is the most challenging step because it requires you to concentrate on one powerful benefit that will be unique to you and be most meaningful to the Customer.

Once you've identified your USP, make sure you test it with your Customers, valued advisors and other important stakeholders. Then, make sure that everyone in your company knows it, believes in it and lives it.

By the way, we'll say it again, please identify the USP for both your company *and* yourself. You are as much a brand as Nike or Nestlé. Build the brand called You. No-one else will. What's more, in a time of increasing layoffs, downsizing and outsourcing, you never know when you may become a self-employed entrepreneur. A powerful *Brand-You* will assist you enormously.

The Third Leg of Bednight Marketing: Use your USP as a Magnet to Customers. Your first challenge is to let go of your inhibitions and assume the Leadership stance. Above all, make the decision now and act.

Okay, you know your Customers and your USP. Now you need to use your USP to draw Customers to you like a Magnet. And your first challenge is to let go of your inhibitions. They have no role to play in the delivery of Spectacular Customer Service. It's not easy. Our natural inclination is to retreat behind the walls of our comfort zone. But if you want to become a Magnet to Customers, you have to do what the Customer wants, not what you want.

There is an old African saying, "The child that does not cry on its mother's back gets suffocated." In a world of chaos and confusion, the noise is deafening, the choices are mind-numbing and the competition is exploding. If you don't shout your USP clearly from the mountain tops, no-one is going to hear you.

Assume the leadership stance. You know that you know your stuff – otherwise you would not have got this far. So strut your stuff. Walk and talk like a leader. Become known as a leader. Stand up and be counted. Grab every opportunity to profile yourself while making things better and helping the people around you.

Take the high ground and a lot of people will want to be with you because you will be seen as a winner, a mover and a shaker. They'll want some of your magic to rub off on them. Time and time again, people call us after attending our seminars and tell us how effectively this strategy works for them. They tell us that the moment they decided to step up, their lives changed. Yes, change can happen in an instant – once you've made the decision to change. So make it today. Remember, this evening there's a bednight waiting to be sold.

In the world of Bednight Marketing, decisions have to be made on the run. Once the USP has been decided, then it's up to the whole company to use it as a Magnet to Customers. That's the key – staff must be empowered to make the decisions on the ground. Expect them to be occasionally wrong. That's natural. Just course-correct as you go along. At Protea Hotels, frontline staff are encouraged to make decisions. And, as Arthur states, although there have been mistakes, there has never been a mistake so serious that Protea Hotels ever felt even slightly motivated to change their policy on this issue.

Six of the best: Marketers who have been highly creative in becoming a Magnet to Customers.

To illustrate the third leg of Bednight Marketing, we identified six marketers who are using their USP very creatively as a Magnet to Customers. These six examples come from very different categories – which goes to show that it's not what you do, it's how you do it:

Nando's – not just about chicken.

Nando's has a smaller marketing budget than many of its bigger competitors, but they have been very successful in creating humorous, controversial advertising that generates a huge amount of media coverage. As a result, they stand out. It pays to be different.

Pratley Glue – You can bet your life on it.

In a very competitive category, Pratley Glue sticks out. Kim Pratley, the Managing Director of the company, appears in commercials with a tractor suspended above his head, held in place by a chain stuck to a disc with Pratley Glue. While his product may not be unique in its performance, the way he advertises it is.

Steve O. Akinboro, Operations Manager, McDonalds South Africa.

You probably haven't heard of Steve Akinboro. He is a Nigerian who emigrated to the UK twenty years ago. After graduating with a MSc, he joined McDonalds in the UK. Steve rose rapidly through the ranks and then seized the opportunity to help launch McDonalds in South Africa. Today, Steve is Operations Manager of McDonalds in this country. The real reason, though, why we have included Steve in this book is his unique, massively enthusiastic style. When Steve is asked how he's doing, his response is always "super-fantastic" and he means it too. Although Steve is 35 years old, he looks 25 and he makes all those around him feel the same way. His personal vision is: "To be a key player in the development of the McDonalds brand on this planet." Steve's USP of "visionary enthusiasm" is why he is destined for great things. Are you?

Richard Branson and Virgin – Fun and Adventure.

Branson must be the all-time world champion USP Magnet for Customers. His relentless promotions, exploits and press coverage have built Virgin into a global brand that stands for fun and adventure.

Red Bull gives you. . .?

If you're a South African, you know the answer. Red Bull's promotion and advertising has been very effective in turning their USP of "gives you wings" into a Magnet for Customers

Robben Island – From prison to top tourist attraction and international brand of faith and freedom.

Recently, we were in America where we saw an American wearing a Robben Island cap. He told us the highlight of his trip to South Africa was his visit to Robben Island. What an amazing marketing turnaround. It is one of South Africa's top tourist attractions, attracting thousands of people who want to experience its USP of faith and freedom.

What about you? How can you become a Magnet to your Customers? Get some media coverage. Why do you think we're writing this book? If you take the first step, LUCK will step in and help you the rest of the way.

Although we have featured some high profile people and brands, you too can use your USP as a Magnet to your Customers. Get your own signature that makes you memorable. When your name is mentioned to your Customers, they should respond, "She's the one who. . .", or "He's the guy who always. . ." For example, Mike Lipkin's signature is his "Yes!" which he communicates both verbally and on his trademark T-shirt. As many people know Mike as the "Yes! Man" as they know him by name.

Here's another insight: media coverage is more effective than advertising because it's more credible. If the media says something about you and your company, it's seen as true. So what can you do that will make the media write about you or your company? It doesn't matter whether it's the Sunday

Times or the Randburg Sun or the Jakkelspisfontein Gazette.

We'll be honest with you: the main reason for writing this book is not the financial return, it's the media coverage. Just like you, we want to build our brand, in this case Juiced! That's why we've tried to make it so different. So once again, we ask you: how can you use your USP to rise above the crowd.

We also promise you this: if you take the first step with confidence and faith, LUCK will come to your aid. As if by magic, all kinds of extraordinary opportunities and Customers will find you. And by the way, you know what LUCK stands for? Labouring Under Correct Knowledge. Just as FAIL stands for First Action In Learning.

Use the Web. All Customers are becoming e-Customers. How's your personal Website looking?

"The person who responds first and strongest will win. From a business standpoint, the Net is brilliant. There's no risk of being hijacked when you do your shopping. There are no queues. And no store assistant can match Amazon.com's knowledge. The Net allows us to know clients and clients to know us. The Net creates new expectations – instant turnaround time, flawless information, links to related issues, personalization, accurate troubleshooting, total accessibility. What's more, you'll never meet an ignorant, surly, uncaring Website. The Net can't insult or ridicule you. . .yet.

In the business to business market, the Net is removing intermediaries. It's flattening the supply chain, cutting the paper trail and punishing anyone who isn't super-efficient. There is no rest in the new world." Ronnie Apteker

Both of us are a long way from being technocrats. In fact, if anything, we're technopeasants. It doesn't matter. You don't have to know how electricity works to turn on the light. If you have a problem, there's always an electrician to call. We love what the Web does. It's not a really serious, mysterious cyber-technology. It's an everyday tool that is extremely useful, lots of fun and an extraordinary way to reach thousands of people instantaneously.

The good news is that you can also create your own Website very inexpensively. It won't be able to do everything the Disney Website can do, but it can do everything you need it to do. Mike's Website, for example, cost him less than R12 000 to set up and costs less than R3 000 a month to maintain. It was voted one of the best small business Websites in South Africa by Business Day. For his investment, he gets about 2 000 hits a week. Or 8 000 hits a month. Or 100 000 hits a year. He estimates that at least 30% of his turnover in 2000 will come directly or indirectly from the Web. What's more, thousands of the people visiting **www.mikelipkin.com** leave their addresses. Mike's e-database, therefore, empowers him to communicate constantly with his e-Prospects. So get connected. In the world of Bednight Marketing, you cannot afford not to be.

Make Raving Fans who generate massive Word-of-Mouth advertising for you.

Ken Blanchard, the well known management consultant and author, coined the term, "Raving Fans." A Raving Fan is someone who is so impressed with your Spectacular Customer Service that he raves about you to whoever he meets. After your immediate family, Raving Fans are unquestionably the most valuable people in your life. You know why? Because they are walking, talking live commercials for you and for your service. Raving Fans will ensure that you are successful.

Your livelihood and our livelihood depend on the number of Raving Fans we can generate. Juiced! will only be a success if sufficient readers like it enough to become Raving Fans. So how many Raving Fans do you have? How many of your Customers right now are walking around raving about you to their friends, family and colleagues. Are you even consciously pursuing this objective? We promise you, if all you take out of this entire book is the drive to create Raving Fans, then you will achieve extraordinary success.

There is no easy way to Juice your Customers. You have to stay in front of their faces, live in their minds and romance their hearts relentlessly. Out of sight, out of mind, out of business.

Bednight Marketing is not a one night stand. It is a never-ending commitment to Juicing your Customers. There are many people who are good marketers some of the time. But that's not good enough. You have to be an outstanding marketer all of the time. *And that means more than half of your business time must be spent in front of Customers* – in person, by phone, by snail mail or by e-mail.

Both of us are addicted to being in front of our clients' faces. Not only do we love it, but we know what we're achieving: we're staying at the top of their shopping list so that when they come into the market, we're the one they call. We want to own their frontal lobes. We want to be synonymous with our industries. So when you think hospitality, we want you to think Protea Hotels. When you think sales training and motivation, we want you to think Mike Lipkin. And, of course, when you think about Spectacular Customer Service books, we want you to think about getting Juiced!

So are you using all the means at your disposal to live in your Customers' minds and romance their hearts relentlessly? Or are you playing second fiddle to your competition? Remember, in the world of Bednight Marketing, once an opportunity is gone, it's gone. It isn't coming back. What's more, and here's the real issue, if you miss this opportunity, you miss all the opportunities downstream that this opportunity would have generated. Hmmm, another thing to make you think.

Part Three

A mistake may be the best thing you ever make. A crisis may be the ultimate gift. As long as you recover magnificently. It's not the mistake or crisis that counts. It's how you make the Customer feel afterwards.

Think back over the past three months, the past six months, the past year. Think about the three biggest mistakes you've made in serving Customers. Now, write down your mistakes, one underneath the other, in a column on the left-hand side of a page. Next to each mistake listed in that column, write down what action you took to rectify the mistake. Next to each action, write down how the Customer felt afterwards – supported by evidence, not just your opinion of how he or she felt. Finally, write down what you learnt about Customer Service through the mistake or crisis.

First of all, we hope you've made some big mistakes. A person who doesn't make mistakes doesn't make anything. Secondly, we hope you actually did this exercise. Do not proceed any further until you've completed this task. Come on, it's quick and easy! Now, if you've done the exercise, what was the result? What action did you take? How did the Customer feel? How effectively did you recover? Did you strengthen the relationship because of the mistake? Or did you offend, annoy and drive the Customer away? Did you rise to the challenge? Or did you give in to the pressure and to the stress of the moment? As you think back, are you proud of yourself and of your company? Or does even remembering the event still embarrass you? Did you see the mistake as a gift or a curse? Most importantly, what did you learn? How did you grow? How did the mistake make your team better?

How are you doing so far? If this was a test and we reviewed your responses to these questions, how would your overall performance rate out of ten? Let's ask you some more key Crisis Management questions: how many times have you had to rectify a problem that you didn't cause in the first place? How many times have you thought to yourself, "This is so unfair"? How many times have Customers "over-reacted" to a mistake or problem? How many times have you lost your cool because the Customer lost his cool? How often have you carried a mistake around with you for days before you let it go? In fact, right now, are you still carrying a grudge because someone shouted at you or insulted you in a moment of temper? Read on. . .

The guiding principle for Spectacular Customer Service must be: these are the rules. Now, let's see what we have to do to solve your challenge and make you happy. We learnt this principle from two monks and a girl.

Here's a lovely story that illustrates the need to be flexible, act and move on: Once upon a time, two monks were on their way back to their monastery when they came to a strongly flowing river which they would have to cross. Both of the monks were big, powerful men, so crossing the river did not pose a problem for them. As they were about to cross, however, they noticed a frail young girl standing about fifty metres downstream on the same side. She looked very afraid because she knew she could not cross the river by herself and night was falling.

The first monk looked at the young girl and decided not to help her because, when he become a monk, he vowed never to touch a woman. The second monk looked at the young girl and became concerned for her safety. He knew that if he didn't help her, she would have to spend the night alone next to the river until it subsided the following morning. He balanced his vows of celibacy against the wellbeing of a fellow human being. He knew that if he didn't help her, and something horrible happened to her, he would never be able to live with himself.

He called to the young girl, put her on his shoulders and carried her across the river. The moment he reached the other side, he put her down and bade her farewell. Then, together with his companion, he continued on the journey.

Five hours later, as the moon rose high in the sky, the first monk said to his companion, "You should be ashamed of yourself. You violated your vows of celibacy by carrying that woman across the river." The second monk replied calmly and simply, "Yes, but I let go of her five hours ago. You're still carrying her around." Makes you think doesn't it? Rules are important. We need them to guide our behaviour. But good judgement, interdependence, decisiveness, adaptability, personal responsibility and flexibility are as important. What are you still carrying around in your head?

Too much sanity is madness.

Please tell us, why did Kamikaze pilots wear crash helmets?

Seriously, if you take nothing else away from this book, take this message: Some of the worst words you can ever say to a Customer are "That's our policy" or "Those are our rules".

The moment you utter those words, you are telling the Customer that he does not count. You are telling him categorically that you and your company cannot and will not give him what he wants. You are saying categorically that you and your company follow a "one size fits all" approach. And, in the age of mass-customization, that approach is corporate suicide. Rules do bring sanity to the often chaotic process of running an organization, but too much sanity is madness.

Achtung, ukuXwayisa, Warning, Waarskuwing: Sixteen things that really annoy Customers and lead to Crises:

Here are some everyday mistakes that many companies make in serving their Customers. These mistakes alone can alienate Customers or they can lead to more serious crises that drive Customers away:

- *When Customers are bounced from person to person.*
- *When staff appear uninterested in serving Customers.*
- *When Customers have to struggle to be acknowledged.*
- *When staff attend to their personal calls while Customers wait.*
- *Hidden costs that inflate the original price.*
- *When Customers are called VIPs and then treated very poorly.*
- *When staff chew gum while attending to Customers.*
- *When Customers find company policies and procedures are impossible to understand.*
- *When Customers are made to feel ignorant because companies use industry jargon.*
- *When Customers are confronted with staff whose body language shouts, "It's not my problem!"*
- *When a promise is made to call a Customer back and nothing happens.*
- *When appointments with Customers are cancelled.*
- *When a Customer's car has more problems after a maintenance check than it had before it went in.*

- *When a Customer is told to "calm down".*
- *When staff answer their cell phones while meeting with Customers.*
- *When potato chip bags have more air than chips.*

Think about your business: what everyday mistakes are you making that could be driving Customers away?

Obliterate the word "wrong" from your personal vocabulary. It is a highly destructive word that hurts, demoralizes and angers others.

Yup, it's tough being in Customer Service. In fact, we believe that Customer Service is really frustration management. It means always being friendly and courteous to people who are not always friendly and courteous. Here's the bottom line: the Customer is not always right. But the Customer is always the Customer. Your challenge and our challenge is how to manage the relationship when something goes wrong. At the end of the day, it really doesn't matter who is wrong. What matters is how you make it right. In fact, we strongly recommend that you obliterate the word "wrong" from your personal vocabulary. It is a highly destructive word that hurts, demoralizes and angers others. If you doubt what we're saying, go and tell ten people that they're wrong, and see what their response is. We believe that people are never "wrong". They just have differences in perception and opinion.

In our work in the hospitality and motivation industries, we have experienced so many organizations that actually appear to enjoy proving Customers wrong. They get a perverse sense of pleasure and power from being "right". Monopolies and certain municipal or government entities seem to specialize in this activity. But we also experience this negative phenomenon throughout the private sector. The problem is especially prevalent at frontline level where staff are rule bound. They are not trained or even encouraged to be flexible. The result is the ultimate lose-lose situation. The Customer is angered, annoyed and alienated. The frontline service provider becomes even more negative and Customer-Unfriendly. And the company continues to move backwards. Here's our message: the moment you get into "rights and wrongs", you've lost the goodwill and trust of the Customer. You've introduced conflict and antagonism into the relationship. Both supplier and Customer become defensive and closed. The good energy flow dries up. And the Customer begins hunting for another partner.

If we said to you right now that we would help you flow through any mistake and use it to make the Customer love you, would you want to know more? We can hear you shouting YES! YES! YES! So let's explore the art of Customer Service Crisis Management together.

What is a Customer Service Crisis? Any time a Customer becomes upset because she believes that something that should have been done hasn't been done.

Let's look at this definition of a Customer Service Crisis:

Any time a Customer becomes upset: For it to be a crisis, the Customer must be upset. She may express her upset state as anger, irritation, disappointment or alarm. The point here is that her expectations have been destroyed to the point of causing her distress.

Because she believes that: It doesn't matter what actually happened, what matters is what the Customer believes happened. Perception is reality. Everything is open to interpretation. It's the point of view of the Customer that counts.

Something that should have been done hasn't been done: Either something literally wasn't done. Or it was done in a way that didn't satisfy the Customer. Or the Customer had a preconception of the kind of service she was going to receive and received something different. The point here is that there is a disconnect between what the Customer wanted and what the Customer got.

One more thing: Customer Service crises have the potential to escalate rapidly. Like a brushfire fanned by a hot wind, they can wipe out your business in a matter of moments. Bad news travels fast. People talk a lot about all those who they believe have done them wrong. In fact, in South Africa, it's our favourite pastime.

A warning: silence isn't golden, it's brown. When your Customer goes quiet, you're deep in the stinky stuff.

As bad as an irate or angry Customer may be, a silent one is far, far worse. When someone goes quiet after an unsatisfactory service experience, it means that they've made the decision to walk away. It means they no longer believe that any action or words will make any kind of difference. Worst of all, when someone goes silent, it means they've either mentally or emotionally removed themselves from the situation, or they're so angry they'd rather stay quiet than rant and rave. Think about those times when you been served so badly that you no longer wish to have anything to do with the company or organization serving you. Think about those times when you've decided to give up on someone or something. Isn't there a point when you retreat into yourself, compose yourself and focus on getting as far away from this person or place as possible?

Any psychiatrist will tell you that the kiss of death for any relationship between two people is when one of them goes silent. When the flow of communication stops, so does everything else. So, contrary to conventional wisdom, silence does not mean consent. It means total and utter contempt.

If an upset Customer is the first phase of losing a

Customer, anger is the second and silence is final. Whatever happens, therefore, keep the Customer talking. Silence isn't golden, it's brown.

What's your Customer Service Crisis Management Strategy?

Do you even have one? Let us ask you this vital question: Do you have a clearly defined, simple action-oriented Customer Service Crisis Management Strategy in your company? If you are one of the rare few who answered "yes" to this answer, here's our next question: Are you and all your colleagues totally familiar with this policy? If you are among the 1% of all organizations who still answered "yes" to this question, here's the next question: Are your frontline people highly motivated to apply this strategy to the delight and joy of your Customers? If you answered "yes" to this question, we promise you that you are either number one or number two in your market.

There are many companies who talk the good talk about Customer Service. All the right words are in their mission statement or in their advertising and promotional literature. But they have not made Spectacular Customer Service an integral part of their corporate conduct. It's a *"should have"* not a *"must have"*. Their people are trained to be technically competent. They are shown how to interface with a computer or a machine or a tool. But computers and machines and tools are not emotional; they aren't irrational; they aren't psychologically insecure. Customers are. Even when a company may have done everything right, a Customer Service crisis may still arise because the Customer is emotionally challenged on that day, or because a Customer has different information that day, or because a Customer changes her mind that day. If that should happen, what strategy would you immediately adopt to resolve the crisis quickly, elegantly and effectively?

A classic Customer Service crisis as illustrated by the case of Gary Go-Getter and the unavailable table.

Gary Go-Getter was a truly impressive man. As the founder and Chief Executive of the highly successful Make-It-Happen Conference Company, he was a tireless networker. Go-Getter was always in front of a Customer or Prospect. He knew that personal contact was the most powerful way to make the sale and win the business. Every day Gary would lunch an important Prospect or Customer at one of his favourite restaurants.

One Wednesday not so long ago, Go-Getter woke up in a state of great anticipation and excitement. A Prospect whom he had been courting for months, Belinda Bigbucks, finally agreed to have lunch with him. Gary whistled to himself as he shaved his handsome face. "You beauty!" he thought, "You've got her right where you want her! Yes!" he said to himself in the mirror as he thought of the sale that he was about to make that afternoon. He put on his finest Italian fully imported suit, his ultimate Yellow power-tie and his freshly starched pure Egyptian white cotton shirt. To round off his immaculate appearance, he slipped his feet into his handmade Brazilian brogues. As he arrived at work, he asked his secretary to confirm the table by the wall, next to the window, overlooking the ocean, in the far right-hand corner of the Seven Seas restaurant. Seven Seas was regarded as the finest seafood restaurant in South Africa. The 5-star Empress Hotel, in whose building the restaurant was located, owned the Seven Seas. The Seven Seas was the jewel in The Empress's crown and the General Manager of the Empress was personally responsible for the restaurant. Anyone who was anyone wanted to be seen dining in this exemplary eating establishment. Reservations for lunch and dinner had to be made weeks in advance. Go-Getter congratulated himself on his foresight in booking this table every Wednesday in anticipation of lunching Prospects like Belinda Bigbucks.

Like the true professional he was, Go-Getter arrived at the restaurant at 12h25, twenty minutes ahead of time. He wanted to make sure everything was perfect, compose himself and visualize the success of this lunch meeting in advance. As he entered the Seven Seas, Go-Getter was greeted by the maitre d', a tall, stiff-looking man in his late fifties who spoke as though he was rehearsing for a part in a Shakespearian play. Gary felt a little uncomfortable because he had never seen this maitre d' before. "Will you be dining with us today?" he asked Gary gratuitously. "No," thought Gary, irritated by the totally unnecessary question, "I'm here to bungee jump!" Instead, he just said, "Yes, of course, the name is Gary Go-Getter. Table for two. What's happened to James?" he asked the maitre d', referring to the man who usually greeted him at the door. The maitre d' glanced at him and replied without expression, "He went back to Burundi last Friday. I have been transferred here from The Island Restaurant until a new manager can be found." Then he looked at the register, nodded his head, put a line through Go-Getter's name and asked Gary to follow him.

To Go-Getter's shock and indignation, the maitre d' showed him to a table by the kitchen, just out of range of the swinging door. As the maitre d' pulled out the chair and motioned for Gary to sit down, Go-Getter said, "This is not the table I booked. I booked the table I always sit at." Then Go-Getter turned and pointed to the table by the window, next to the wall, overlooking the ocean in the far right-hand corner of the room. "That's the table I want," said Gary. "I'm sorry," the maitre d' replied, "That table is reserved for a very important Customer." Go-Getter exploded, "And what do you think I am? I come here every single week and I sit at that table over there, not at this insulting table over here. My secretary even confirmed that I would have that table overlooking the ocean." He took a breath and then continued in a loud, angry tone, "You don't understand, I have a very important Customer coming here in twenty minutes. I have a lot at stake. And I'm not going to allow you to screw it all up for me. Do you hear me?" The maitre d' just looked at Gary with a blank expression that seemed to say, "You're overreacting for nothing. Stop being so childlike." Instead, he just said, "I'm sorry, sir, but this is the only table we have available. All the others have been reserved. I'm afraid you'll just have to settle for this one today."

What would you have done if you were Gary? What could you have done if you were the maitre d'? What could the Seven Seas Restaurant or the Empress Hotel have done to prevent this debacle in the first place?

So, what *would* you have done if you were Gary? One thing is for sure, Gary had a right to be massively angry. He was the model Customer. He was a regular, he did everything right, including confirming the booking and arriving early. As indicated, he exploded. But he didn't have the option of going silent and walking away. His Prospect was about to arrive. So Gary could have calmed down and reasoned with the maitre d', or he could have suggested other options. The bottom line is that Gary was treated terribly – just as all of us have been at one time or another.

What *could* the maitre d' have done? Everything. He should have known that Gary was a loyal Customer. How? Well Gary knew the name of the previous manager. He also told the maitre d' that he was a regular. Any maitre d' worth his salt should also have seen Gary as the kind of very successful businessperson who is the backbone of any upmarket restaurant. The maitre d' could therefore have shifted the other Guests around. He could even have shifted a couple tables around. He could have apologised to Gary and asked him to wait in the bar while he repaired the situation. Even if it was impossible to give Gary the table by the window, he could have allocated him a table in the middle of the room – one step up from the table by the kitchen.

Most importantly, what the maitre d' should have known, and what all of us should know, is that his task was really to give Gary massive recognition and respect. He did neither. Gary, as you've read, is a high profile kind of guy. He likes fine clothes, fine food and socializing with other successful people. So let's say that the maitre d' was forced to place Gary in the middle of the room. First of all, he could have apologized profusely. He could have provided Gary with a free bottle of fine wine. He could have invited the chef to come out and chat with Gary in front of Belinda Bigbucks. He could have showered him with Spectacular Service throughout the lunch. He could have provided them with complimentary chocolates or a half bottle of champagne at the end of the lunch.

Our key message to you here is that what the maitre d' did was unforgivable. He committed the capital offence of Customer Service: he compounded the initial error of not giving Gary the desired table with a shocking lack of follow-up. We all know that mistakes are sometimes inevitable. But once the mistake has been made, it must be acknowledged and resolved with maximum care, creativity and speed. The maitre d' could have turned Gary around totally if he responded appropriately.

What should the Empress Hotel have done to prevent the debacle from occurring in the first place? Well, they could have had a clear strategy in place to handle this kind of situation quickly and elegantly. They could have ensured that only Customer-friendly people were allowed to work at their restaurants. They could have trained the maitre d' to apply the kind of attitude that respects and recognizes Customers.

They could have a specific guideline for the treatment of loyal Customers. They could have a mandate in place where the maitre d' would be required to call the Empress's General Manager in extreme situations like this.

We all know one thing is absolutely certain: in the very, very near future, all of us will be faced with a crisis. It's not important who caused the crisis. The only thing that's important is that it's our responsibility to resolve it. Don't try to resolve crises in an ad hoc kind of way. The essence of spectacular Customer Service is being prepared. So start thinking about your Customer Service crisis management now! In the next section, we will give you a blueprint to work with, but you need to customize it to your business.

Once again, though, this story proves that the person in charge of the operation in the field is the number one reason why an operation succeeds or fails. You can have the finest systems, infrastructure and strategies in the world, but if the individual-in-charge is negligent, everything else falls apart.

The Gillis-Lipkin Specialized 7-Step Guide to Customer Service Crisis Resolution:

The Gillis-Lipkin definition of Specialize: *the art of making a Customer feel special even after he or she has been disappointed, offended or annoyed.*

Step 1: **Apologize immediately with genuine empathy and caring.**

Step 2: **Take responsibility. Take control. Don't badmouth the company and don't go hunting for blame in front of the Customer. Dance, don't fight.**

Step 3: **Do whatever you can to fix the problem or resolve the situation immediately. Be crisis-ready.**

Step 4: **Have a resource-in-reserve that can be applied when and where it's needed fast. Bring on the Super-Subs.**

Step 5: **Minimize the Customer's inconvenience or discomfort financially, emotionally and physically. Take the sting out of the negative experience. Manage your Customer's memory.**

Step 6: **Follow up within 24 hours. Make another deposit into the memory bank account.**

Step 7: **Evaluate the service delivery process and implement changes to prevent the mistake happening again. Get better, not bitter. "What can we learn from this?" Stay positively paranoid.**

Through hard experience as both service providers and Customers, we have formulated our Specialized 7-Step Guide to Customer Service Crisis Resolution. As we share our Guide with you, ask yourself how you can adapt it to your business. As far as this Guide is concerned, our definition of copyright is that you have the right to copy. Apply it to your business as soon as possible and let us know the results by visiting www.mikelipkin.com and leaving us a message.

And by the way, this Guide can probably be used to resolve many of the crises that occur in your personal relationships. You know why? Because, as we said at the very beginning of this book, ultimately everyone is your Customer. Your spouse, your relatives, your friends and your colleagues all require service from you. They also all pay you in some way or another. They may not make deposits into your financial bank account but they certainly make deposits into your emotional bank account. See everyone as your Customer and you'll never take anyone for granted.

Before we explore the 7-step Guide, there are two core principles that we want to share with you. These two principles drive the entire book. They are the two vital factors of all spectacular Customer Service:

The Telkom 1023 Principle: keep telling the Customer what's happening. Ignorance comes from being ignored, so does irritation, anger and anxiety. Think about it: how do you feel when you're not getting what you want and no-one is telling you why? When you think you're being ignored, disregarded or forgotten, what's your attitude towards your service provider? Hmm, we thought so.

So practise the Telkom 1023 Principle. Call 1023 on your landline right now. If it is not answered by a live human being, you will hear a voice that tells you, "Your call will be answered in approximately two minutes and nineteen seconds." A few seconds later, you will get another message, "Your call will be answered in approximately 55 seconds." And so on until your call is answered. As a result of their constant updating and communication, we're prepared to hold on. However, if we had heard the usual "Your call is important to us", we would have hung up about 40 seconds into the waiting period.

Walt Disney does the same thing at Disney World in Orlando, Florida, USA. Every few yards, they tell their Guests who are standing in queues how long they have to wait for the next ride. The moment people know what's happening, they get an extra measure of patience. But if they're kept in the dark or if they feel as if they're being maltreated, all of their patience evaporates immediately.

The message here is that, if you keep telling your Customers what's happening, they are far more likely to forgive you for any mishaps and remain loyal to you. If you don't, they won't. It's that simple. So why don't we talk to our Customers? On to the second principle. . .

When the bad stuff hits the fan, the outstanding performers run towards it with urgency and drive. The mediocre ones run away as fast and as far as

they can. A crisis is a moment of truth: you can make it a moment of magic or a moment of misery.

Jason Levine, CEO of Circus Enterprises Inc, was heard saying to one of his problematic frontline employees, "Why can't you solve our Customer's problems? Is it ignorance or is it apathy?" The employee looked at Levine skeef and replied, "I don't know and I don't care."

It's amazing. You can always tell the champions by what direction they choose in a crisis. The champions relish a challenge. They go looking for the problems. Somehow, they're always there when you need them. And they're not stressed or uptight. They're in the High Performance Zone. They are fully focused on the solution. They act with controlled urgency. They know that they're building their character and maximising their potential. They're in flow with the problem. They don't struggle or curse. They love testing themselves in extreme situations. These are the members of the Customer Service A-Team. These are the people you want by your side when you need them most. And these are the kind of people who populate South Africa's best service companies. Look around you, what kind of company do you work in?

On the other hand, the mediocre performers become invisible in a crisis. They look away and run away until someone else makes the problem go away. These are the people with weak problem-solving muscles. These are the cowards who die a thousand deaths every week. These are the people who just don't get it: life is about solving problems. The only people who don't have to solve problems live in a cemetery. What's more, the more problems you solve, the easier it gets. Problems are the gymnasium of your mind. The more problems you lift off Customers' shoulders, the tougher you become mentally, emotionally and even physically because you stop worrying so much.

So from today, whatever happens, run towards the

problem, even if you're not quite sure how to handle it. If you stay open and committed to helping the Customer, the answers will come to you just as you need them. No guts, no gold. And what is courage after all? It's nothing but the willingness to face your own fear.

If you are the kind of person who may have run from problems in the past, kill your Tokoloshe (demon) now. Because if you don't, we promise you it's going to kill you. We know about the feelings of shame and guilt that cripple people who don't do what they know they have to do. Nothing is worse than the knowledge that you gave less than you could have given. Regret will make you sick. Right now, take this vow to yourself (by the way, even if you believe that you're a "run-to-the-problem-kind-of-person", renew this vow to yourself):

"I do whatever it takes to solve my Customer's problems. I find a way or make a way even when others say there is no way. I care deeply about my team members. I care deeply about my Customers. I put myself on the line every day. I love the pressure. I inspire the people around me. I always give more than I take. I'm ready for anything. I choose to be excited right now because I have the opportunity to serve. Yes!!"

How do you feel as you read these words? Empowered? Excited? Enthusiastic? Energized? Encouraged? Or all of these? You've just discovered the power of self talk – the words you use to communicate with yourself. Keep these words with you at all times. Write them down in your diary. Say them to yourself in the tough moments. Use them to motivate yourself to run towards the problem, never away. And help others do the same.

The bottom line is that a Customer Service crisis is a moment of truth for you and your company. It's when your resolve and resources are tested to the maximum. How you choose to handle the Customer Service Crisis will make it a moment of magic or a moment of misery. Remember, it's always your choice.

Okay, now let's have some fun with the Gillis-Lipkin 7-Step Guide to Customer Service Crisis Resolution:

Step 1: Apologize immediately with genuine caring.

"Don't they teach you how to apologize in Lawyer School? Because you suck at it!" Erin Brockovich

Every single day, South Africans are given massive amounts of stress. They are threatened, overloaded, insulted, ignored, conned, disappointed and discouraged. And that's just for starters. That's why so many of us overreact to the "small stuff". It's the last straws that are breaking our spirits. It's got to the point for many of us where we almost expect things to wrong before they do, so that when they do go wrong, we can say to the people around us, "I told you so". The reality is that many of us are running out of emotional gas to deal with the difficulties that surround us.

Remember this first truth: people lose their tempers when they don't know how to handle a situation. They lose their tempers when they are in emotional pain themselves. They also lose their tempers to camouflage their fear. That's why it's so important for us not to lose our tempers when a Customer loses their temper with us. It's really just a cry for help and support. If you are in the business of dealing with Customers, therefore, know this second truth: you are a psychologist. You are there to calm Customers and make them feel better through genuine empathy and caring. Remember this old Chinese saying: *Person who loses temper, loses Customer.*

You can't fake it.

Customers don't care how much you know, until they know how much you care. You cannot fake it. Customers can sense immediately when it's not coming from the heart. Think of those times when you've been served by someone who is giving you a fake apology. Can't you tell that they don't really mean it? You know why? 90% of all communication is non verbal. Words account for 10%. Voice counts for 40%. Body language counts for 50%. Every part of you must commit to the apology.

What happens if you don't apologize? Doesn't the Customer become even more uptight? But what happens if you do apologize immediately? In the majority of cases, doesn't the Customer begin to relax immediately? Sometimes the Customer even takes some of the responsibility himself. You know why? Because he has already achieved his most important goal: he has received recognition. You've shown him that he actually matters. You've given him a shot of significance.

Always remember that the Customer's credibility and ego are on the line. If you puncture his ego or endanger his credibility, you will never be forgiven. On the other hand, if you honour his ego and credibility even though there has been a screw-up, you'll probably end up making a Customer for life.

When you do apologize, do not say, "I'm terribly sorry". The word "terrible" is really a terrible word. Rather say, "I'm truly sorry" or "We really apologize". If you really want to build strong Rapport with an upset Customer, say, "If I had been treated like you were, I would have never have been as reasonable as you're being! I would have gone ballistic." Watch the Customer. You'll really see a change in attitude – for the better.

Step 2: Take responsibility. Don't badmouth the company, don't go hunting for blame in front of the Customer and don't try to prove the Customer is at fault. Dance with the Customer, don't fight.

How many times has a Customer Service representative apologized to you and then badmouthed or blamed someone else in his company? How did you feel about both the person and his company when this happened? Did you lose more than a little trust in both of them? Also, didn't you feel just a little bit uncomfortable when the person washed his dirty linen in front of you?

Here's our message: resist the temptation to blame others, even if you have to resolve a problem that had nothing to do with you in the first place. As far as the Customer is concerned, you are the company. So don't wobble. Take charge. Never say "They." Instead use "We" and "Us". Delighting Customers is tough enough as it is, don't waste energy searching for someone to blame. And you know what? Even if you do find someone to blame, how does that help you? It just makes you angrier. What's more, if you confront the person you're blaming, you'll probably just make another enemy who is not going to help you out of a crisis next time around. All your energy should be constructively invested in repair and progress.

Yes, this step takes guts. It requires the caring and the courage to take ownership of the situation. That's why so few people are exceptional Customer Service providers in the first place. They don't have the self-belief to stand tall in the storm. Instead, they run for cover and hope that someone else will eventually resolve the situation. But we know that you are not this type of person, otherwise you would not have made it this far. Are we right?

If you are successful at proving the Customer wrong, you've just succeeded in losing her and pushing your entire company dangerously close to bankruptcy.

Let's ask you another vital question: have you ever dealt with a representative of a company who has tried to prove that you're the one who made the mistake in the first place, and that's why there's now a problem? How did that make you feel? Didn't those words fan the flames of your fury? Know this: if you are successful at proving the Customer wrong, you've just succeeded in losing her and pushing your entire company dangerously close to bankruptcy. You know why? Because she will tell about a hundred people about your lack of tact or caring. And they will spread the bad word as well. So whatever happens, dance with the Customer, don't fight.

Let's ask you this question: in a crisis, what do people crave more than anything else? Leadership, right? So take control. A mistake or a crisis is a superb opportunity to build your leadership muscles. Be strong. Be decisive. Assume the position and the points will come later.

Here's an unquestionable fact: Customers greatly admire people with courage because they are so rare. Courage is also the twin of integrity. And all of us want to deal with people who have both of those qualities. That's why a mistake or Customer Service crisis can be so healthy: if you demonstrate your caring, courage and integrity, you'll prove to the Customer why she should keep giving you her business.

The next time you have to fix a mistake or resolve a crisis, don't see it as yet another hassle or source of stress. See it as an opportunity to strengthen your mental, emotional and communication muscles. In your mind, celebrate your crises. They've been sent to grow you. And remember: you are never given anything you can't handle, although it may sometimes appear like it.

Step 3: Do whatever you can to fix the problem or resolve the situation immediately. Be crisis-ready.

The single-minded outcome that drives all interaction with the Customer must be:

> *How can we immediately resolve the Customer's problem fairly and intelligently to our mutual satisfaction?*

Once you've apologized and taken responsibility, your main mission now is to fix the problem immediately. The words that the Customer is waiting to hear are, "Here's what we're going to do to make it right" or "Here's how we're going to give you what you want" or "If we did this, would that be OK for you?" or "We're fixing the problem and we'll have a solution for you in a moment."

Our point here is that you must take meaningful, bold action to eliminate the Customer's grievances as soon as possible. The longer you allow the Customer to think about how he is prejudiced by your poor service, the more difficult it is to turn him around. Think about your Customer Service challenges. How long does it take you and your company to resolve a Customer's problem? Do you move at the speed of sound or the speed of a snail? Know this truth about human beings: if we think that we are the victims of any kind of wrongdoing, we will find more and more reasons to back up our beliefs. So the longer you allow a Customer to stew, the more agitated the Customer will become. What begins as a niggle very quickly explodes into a Nagasaki.

Imagine that in one minute you will be confronted by a Customer Service crisis. Are you trained and empowered to deal with it yourself? Or do you need to consult with a colleague? How long will that take? How will you look to the Customer? How will the Customer feel? How likely is it that the crisis will be resolved to the Customer's satisfaction?

Think about your own experiences: how do you feel when you're told, "I can't make the decision, I need to call my supervisor"? We believe that there are definitely times when a more senior person will be required to resolve the situation, but the Second Platinum Rule of Spectacular Customer service is: Empower the frontline person to resolve the situation. We know it's easier said than done. It requires training. It requires confidence. It requires support. It requires the willingness to live with mistakes. But the upside is enormous. Give people responsibility and they will rise to the occasion. Both of us have seen this phenomenon time and time again. Yes, there have been times when it has cost us money. However, in the vast majority of cases, our people have made us massively proud. More importantly, their empowerment has freed us up to concentrate on other initiatives to build our businesses.

Step 4: Have a fresh resource-in-reserve that can be applied when and where it's needed fast. Bring on the Super-Subs.

No matter how well trained you or your staff are, you can only take so much pressure and stress before you crack. Customer Service providers need to be constantly supported and rejuvenated. No-one can take relentless, intense friction and confrontation without a break.

All of us have been the victims of service delivered by people who are way past breaking point. They make mistakes. They are rude. They are negligent. They become very impatient very quickly. They look at their Customers with contempt and even dislike. Their attitude seems to be "This would be a bloody nice place to work if it wasn't for the Customers." Can you identify with these comments?

That's why we believe in having a resource-in-reserve that can step in at any time and defuse a potentially negative situation. This resource-in-reserve may be required when there is a confrontation between Customers and frontline staff. The frontline service provider may have slipped into an argument or stalemate with the Customer. He may be so close to the problem that he can't see the wood for the trees. By coming in fresh, the resource-in-reserve can resolve the issue fast and effectively. It's just like Super 12 or Test Rugby: late in the game, when the starting players are tiring, the Super-Subs – the impact players – take to the field to add fresh energy to the team.

Frontline staff must see this resource-in-reserve as a powerful positive. If the Super-Subs are called in, it's not a reflection on the frontline person's ability to cope. It's simply a means of facilitating progress to the benefit of the Customer and the company alike, while giving the frontline person a much needed breather and support.

Step 5: Minimize the Customer's inconvenience or discomfort financially, emotionally and physically. Take the sting out of the negative experience. Manage your Customer's memory.

If we said to you right now that we would give you the ultimate secret to Spectacular Customer Service Recovery, you would want to know it, wouldn't you? Well, here it is:

It's not the actual experience that determines a Customer's level of happiness. It's their memory of it.

It's what the Customer takes away with her that determines her delight or demotivation. So even if a mistake is made to the discomfort or inconvenience of the Customer, if you take the sting out of it, it can still be a highly motivational memory for the Customer. Let's go back to Gary Go-Getter. If the maitre d' had recovered magnificently, Go-Getter would have become an even more loyal Customer.

So from this moment on, focus on Customer memory management. If you or your organization make a mistake, ensure that the Customer's memory of the experience is a pleasant one. Remember the Law of Recency: human beings tend to remember the last event that happened to them. So, for example, if you're making a speech, close off on a high. If you're serving a meal, make sure the coffee is hot and freshly brewed. If you're managing a project, make sure you conclude it immaculately. At the end of every interaction, shake someone's hand, look him in the eye and tell him with genuine delight what a pleasure it was to serve him.

Just like you, we're in business to make a profit by giving our Customers ten times more than they give us. However, when we are clearly at fault, we will do whatever we have to do to ensure that the Customer has a pleasant memory of the experience. This is not the time to economize or save on expenses. If we have to overcompensate the Customer for the mistake, we will and we will do it with passion. If the mistake was the result of negligence by a staff member, we will address the issue later with him. But in the heat of the moment, all that matters is that the Customer leaves us with a very sweet taste in his mouth. It's not how you start but how you finish that counts. Make sure that you deliver your most scintillating, dazzling service when a Customer has been let down. De-stress him, don't distress him.

Do you want to be massively successful? Are you ambitious? Do you want fame and fortune? If you answered yes to any of these questions, know this truth: the fastest way to success, fame and fortune is through a spectacular ability to turn around the most problematic situations. So the next time you're faced with a Customer Service crisis, celebrate – you're about to claim your place at the top. Become known as the Turnaround Queen or King and your future success is assured.

Step 6: Follow up within 24 hours. Make another deposit into the memory bank account.

This is a very simple step. But it is the one step that can make a bigger impression than any other action to give the Customer a Spectacular Service experience. You know why? Because almost no-one does it. When was the last time you received a follow up call from a service provider, especially when they made an initial mistake in serving you?

Try it. The next time you resolve a challenging situation, call the Customer within 24 hours to follow up. Hear the response for yourself. You will be amazed and so will the Customer. However, when you call the Customer, remember that your primary reason for doing so is to make him feel special. Tell him what a pleasure it was to serve him. Let him know how important he is to your business. Tell him with genuine enthusiasm how much you look forward to serving him again. Reaffirm your commitment to his future success.

Depending on what happened and your personal style, you may also send him a letter, card or small gift. Do not e-mail him. E-mails are impersonal and "Unspecial". Furthermore, do not call him from your car or when you don't have much time to speak. Compose yourself, take a deep breath and focus all your energy on "specializing" this Customer.

Step 7: Evaluate the service delivery process and implement changes to prevent the mistake happening again. Get better, not bitter. "What can we learn from this?" Stay Positively Paranoid.

There are certain mistakes that will always happen. It's called the Human Factor. But there are many mistakes that are generated by the service delivery process or rather, the lack of process. Every day, the two of us make mistakes and we fix mistakes. In fact, that's probably what we really are – "The Mistake Masters" or "The Crisis Kings." One of the reasons why we excel in situations where mistakes or crises are occurring is that we've stripped most of the emotion out the equation. After so many years of slipping and sliding our way to success, we now know that mistakes and crises are our real learning experiences. We learn far more from our mistakes than we ever do from our triumphs.

We're not saying it doesn't hurt when something goes wrong and we lose a Customer. In fact, next to a heart attack, that's the most serious thing that could happen to us. Of course we feel the pain and the frustration of not always being able to deliver according to our highest standards. What we are saying is that we cut through the emotion to find the pearl of learning that will make us better in the future, not bitter.

We're also going to tell you something that is as true as life itself: it's good to lose valuable Customers. What's more it's inevitable. Why is it good? Because too many good Customers can make you complacent despite your best efforts to stay hungry and humble. Losing a good Customer is the ultimate wake-up call. It's a relationship Red Bull that will force you to get rid of the disempowering thoughts and processes that led to the loss. You know what the tragedy is though? Many people and many companies just don't get it. They insult the Customer. They rationalize why the Customer is a moron. They refuse to review their operations and, before they know it, they're in deep trouble. They deserve to be. Nothing ever happens that wasn't supposed to happen. What is, is. What was, was. You decide what will be.

The difference between the great ones and the goners is that the great ones don't go into denial and defence. They do the opposite: they open up. They ask themselves and the Customer that has left why it happened. Then they decide it will never happen again and they take action to back up their decisions. You know what else the great ones do? They make it their mission to re-convert the Customer to their companies. Do you? Don't get mad. Get the Customer back.

We learnt the concept of Positive Paranoia from Reg Lascaris, Chairman of the TBWA Hunt Lascaris Advertising Agency – one of South Africa's most successful companies. Lascaris believes that Customer Service is all about being paranoid but not being paralyzed. There always needs to be a fear motivating you to take the service to the next level before you're forced to. But this is the "Good" fear. It's the excitement and adrenalin that fuels all acts of spectacular Customer Service. "Beware the Comfort Zone," says Lascaris, "it's really the holding pen for people about to get fired." Consider yourself warned.

You're not the boss, you're the coach. And you prove how good you are as a coach whenever you help your frontline person grow through an unhappy Customer experience. Coaching is not Confrontation. The employee will treat the Customer the way he is treated by the company.

Let's ask you this question: How well do you coach your people after they've made a mistake? Do you express your agitation and irritation with them? Worse, do you ever lose your temper with them? How do they feel about being coached by you? When you call them to your office, do they dread the encounter? Or do you turn an unhappy Customer experience into a highly constructive learning experience?

As Managing Director of Protea Hotels, Arthur often receives calls from unhappy Guests. Most of the time, Guests call Arthur simply because they are frequent Guests and they care about Protea or they just feel it's the right thing to do. It's very seldom that a Guest calls with an unwarranted issue.

Now it's one thing handling the Guest. It's quite another coaching the staff member that may have led to the Guest complaint. In fact, handling negative feedback in a nurturing way may be the biggest challenge facing anyone in a leadership position. If you handle it poorly, you can damage the service delivery permanently because you associate mistakes with pain and punishment in the mind of the frontline service provider. The moment your staff member asks himself this fatal question, "What happens if I make a mistake again?" it's game over! If your people live in fear of your anger and wrath, they will not be able to serve their Customers with joy and "Gees".

We want to make this point very, very strongly here: no-one has the right to verbally abuse another person under any circumstances whatsoever. This is not just interpersonal respect, it's vital business practice. Lose your temper with someone just once, and you may lose their commitment forever. So from this second onwards, take control of your emotions before they destroy you, your relationships, your business, your career and the careers of the people around you. And here's something else to think about: how many times have you become angry with someone else only to discover that you're the one at fault? How embarrassed and guilty did that make you feel? How did the other person look at you after that event? What was the impact on their performance for the rest of the day or the rest of the week? What was the impact on the colleagues of this staff member who probably went into "self-pity party" mode after your outburst? What was the impact on the overall quality of Customer Service? As you can see, the downward spiral of one unfortunate act is never-ending.

Coaching is not confrontation. One of the main reasons why supervisors and managers don't coach their staff is that they simply haven't been taught the skills. As a result, they avoid doing it. The inappropriate behaviour continues. It becomes habitual. The situation worsens. And the Customer suffers along with the business.

If it's delivered more than 24 hours after the event, the feedback has exceeded its use-by-date. Burn the annual review.

Coaching is continual. We believe in 24x7x365 performance reviews. As you see things happening, coach your people through the game. Do it with the single-minded intent of making your staff member more successful and we promise you that you'll become a great coach.

The key take-home value here is that your performance reviews must be real time. The longer the lag between the act and the appraisal, the more impotent the appraisal will be. In fact, if it's delivered more than 24 hours after the event, the feedback has exceeded its use-by-date.

So don't relegate the most important part of your role as a leader to a once-a-year performance appraisal. In fact, we recommend burning the annual review. It is nothing but a source of animosity and friction. Think about it: for twelve months, you are building a file of all the things that have gone wrong – yes, plus a few that have gone right. Then months after the mistakes, you remind the employee of all the mess-ups he has made. That's an outstanding way to really annoy your people. What's more, even if you give me good feedback, it's going to be overshadowed by all the bad stuff.

Prescription without diagnosis is malpractice. If you keep asking the right questions, your staff members will give themselves the right answers.

After a Guest has called Arthur with a complaint, Arthur will call the staff member involved in the incident. He will tell him about the call and ask him what happened. Then he will ask him whether he believes he acted appropriately at the time. Very often, the staff member will admit that he could have handled the situation differently. Arthur will then ask him what he believes he could have done to pre-empt the problem. With a tiny bit of nudging here and there, most of the time, he will then give Arthur the correct course of action he could have taken. Or, the staff member may sometimes justify his actions. In those instances, Arthur may respond as follows,

"You may very well be right, but the Guest perceived it differently. And Guest perceptions, for better or for worse, are what will make us successful or not. Here's how we could have possibly handled the situation so that the Guest perceived the outcome favourably. . . Do you agree? As a result, this is what I've done for the Guest. I hope you are comfortable with my decision because we don't want to lose the Guest. OK?"

Notice how Arthur handled this delicate matter. His first move was to ask the staff member about their interpretation of the event. If the problem was serious enough, he would have spoken to other people involved in the incident. Without first doing his homework, Arthur could have done some serious damage to the morale of this staff member and to that of his team. In stress-filled moments, all of us run the risk of jumping to incorrect conclusions. We prescribe a course of action that may not fit the circumstances. As a result, the prescription causes more harm than the initial problem in the first place. Remember, prescription without diagnosis is malpractice.

Also, have you noticed how we've written this book? What have we done on almost every page? In fact, what are we doing right now? Aren't we asking questions? Aren't you giving yourself the answers? And aren't you far more likely to believe yourself than you are to believe anybody else trying to lecture or dictate answers to you? *Questions are the answer.* Keep asking the right questions and your staff will give themselves the right answers. What's more, if you're always asking questions, you're always stretching your staff. They are challenging their brains. They're getting into the habit of finding the solutions for themselves. They're continually increasing their independence and their self- reliance. And you're continually increasing the quality of the service your team delivers to your Customers.

Our final words and a final request: be a resource not just a resident. Be a participant not a passenger. And be Juiced not jaded. The two sweetest sounding words in the English language are "Thank you".

Thank you for finishing what you started. If you've stuck with us to the end, we know you've squeezed some Juice out of this book. We hope that we've also inspired you to go out and Juice others. As Nelson Mandela said in his inauguration speech on 10 May 1994, "As you let your own light shine, you unconsciously give others permission to do the same."

Throughout the preceding pages, we have explored the roles of both the organization and the individual in delivering Spectacular Customer Service. On this final page, we'd like to sum it all up as follows:

The organization provides the context, the individual provides the commitment.

So be a resource to all your fellow South Africans, not just a resident. See how many Thank You's you can collect every day. Because that's the true path to real wealth – the gratitude and appreciation by others for your contribution. And just because you don't receive a "Thank You" today, don't stop collecting them tomorrow. If you make a difference to just one person, you've made a difference to the world, one person at a time.

We really, really want your feedback on Juiced! We also want to hear about your examples of Spectacular Customer Service. Tell us by visiting www.mikelipkin.com or fax us on (011) 728-6907.

Finally, if you want to find out how Arthur and Mike can personally help you and your organization deliver Spectacular Customer Service, contact Mike on 083-625-1188 or e-mail him on lipkin@global.co.za

Go well and stay Juiced!

Notes

Notes

Notes